GHOST STATIONS V

BY THE SAME AUTHOR

Ghost Stations

Ghost Stations II

Ghost Stations III

Ghost Stations IV

GHOST STATIONS

V

by

BRUCE BARRYMORE HALPENNY

Casdec Limited

Cover designed by Baron Barrymore Halpenny

GHOST STATIONS

V

First published March 1993

Published by
Casdec Limited
22 Harraton Terrace
Birtley
Chester-le-Street
Co Durham
DH3 2QG

Telephone: 091 410 5556
Fax: 091 410 0229

British Library Cataloguing in Publication Data

Halpenny, Bruce Barrymore
Ghost Stations V
1. Great Britian - Royal Air Force
1914-1918 - 1939-1945
Mystery 2. Airfields - Ghosts
1. Title

ISBN 0 907595 81 2

GHOST STATIONS

V

... TRUE GHOST MYSTERY STORIES ...

My speciality is being right when other people are wrong.
You Never Can Tell - Act 2
George Bernard Shaw (1856 - 1950).
Irish dramatist and critic.

CONTENTS

ACKNOWLEDGEMENTS

Molto Grazie ... as we say in Italy ... Many Thanks. And that goes out to everyone who has helped with Ghost Stations V. All of you that took the time and trouble to write, with either new material or, to say how you had enjoyed Ghost Stations. All of your letters most welcome.

Molto Grazie. Thank you to you all with a special mention for:
Nigel Bailey - Underwood, Leicester.
Dave Benfield - Market Deeping.
Ken Billingham, Sheffield.
Bob Blunden, King's Lynn.
Ken Border, Swindon.
Neville Bowles, Lincoln.
Bundesarchiv, Germany.
Squadron Leader Cunnane, RAF Scampton.
Edward (Herb) Currotte, Campbellton, Canada.
Ron Day, Little Hadham.
J. Diamantakos for the Glenn Miller photographs which were taken by his brother.
Herr Helmut Dreher, Germany.
Mick Fisher, Yorkshire.
Graeme and Janice Garnham, Middleton St George.
Ralph Gilbert, Chelmsford.
Heinz von Hahn, Geneve, Switzerland.
Derek Harrison, Birmingham.,
Betty Hockey, Bournemouth.
Brian Hunter, Rhodesia.
Werner Hoffmann, Germany.
Major Robert Keith Jones, Chelmsford.
Colonel de Jong, Dutch Ministry of Defence.
Squadron Leader Ken Kenton, RAF Rtd., Kassel, Germany.
Desmond Keen, Great Missenden.

J.R. Laming, Sheffield, for photograph (A) at Ossington.
Gamekeeper Phil Longden, Newark.
Wing Commander Martin, Buckinghamshire.
Godfrey Mangion, Malta.
Bob McPhie - Founder The Dodo Bird Club, Canada.
Roy Nettleship for photographs (B) and (C) at Ossington.
Nicky Pearson, Waddington.
Jock Pepper, Binbrook.
David Peel, Durham.
Walt Scott, Scunthorpe.
Carl Schulte, Lausanne, Switzerland.
James Silver, Nottingham.
Derek Smith, Romford.
Flying Officer Brian Stephenson VR, Tyne-and-Wear.
Edward Stott, Cheshire.
Lance Tebbutt, Felixstowe.
Jan Thorpe, Scampton.
Flying Officer Nicky Tilmouth, WRAF, RAF Waddington.
John W. Tilmouth, Whitley Bay.
Alan Waddington, RAF Newton.
Wilbur Wright, Southampton.
Jill Yates, Manchester.
Bill and Barbara Young, London.

With a very special mention for my many Italian friends ... My old and very dear friend Professore Mario Medoro and his very beautiful wife Diana ... At Casa Medoro 'mangiare bene', Dottore Mario, Domenico and Lucia and the bella Signorina Carmela for helping to sort it all out.

Back in cold old England, a very special mention for Doctor Graham Parry for keeping me going against the cold English weather. And last but not least, Maggie for the UK typing.

AUTHOR'S NOTE

In this volume we have ghostly stories and mysteries from far and wide ... stories told for the very first time.

And that is very much so with 'The Dam Buster's Curse' with material and photographs published here for the first time.

And from the many ... chilling and exciting stories .. will unfold the reason why the old wartime and present day airfields are haunted.

As the Church of England crumbles the revival of a pagan religion which first appeared more than 2,500 years ago is sweeping Europe.

Now there are to be women priestesses ... but as a layman the First Book of Epistles says: 'As in all the churches of the saints, the women should keep silence in the churches. For they are not permitted to speak but, should be subordinate, as even the law says. If there is anything they desire to know, let them ask their husbands at home. For it is shameful for a woman to speak in church ... (1 Corinthians 14.34).

But women can ... and do, read my Ghost Stations. And, the bulk of the letters that I receive are from the fairer sex. And talking of sex ... I end my Ghost Stations V with Sex.

Bruce Barrymore Halpenny
Roma
Italia

A man is only as old as the woman he feels.
Groucho Marx (1895 - 1977)
American film comedian.

SPINSTER'S LUCK

In all of my Ghost Stations books I have included a poem or two. And, quite naturally, they all have a haunting theme ... in keeping with Ghost Stations and the old wartime airfields.

But for Ghost Stations V I thought to change the theme and sprinkle a little humour and, include a poem written by Ralph Gilbert, a former mid-upper-gunner in Halifax bombers of 158 Squadron based at Lissett in Yorkshire.

To help pass away the hours, as he scanned the hostile night sky, Ralph would make up poems.

Readers of my Ghost Stations may well recall that in Ghost Stations Book One, the story about 'The Reaper's Bomber', (page 159), that haunted RAF Lissett.

The once busy main entrance at RAF Lissett

The moon was already well up when Halifax X-Xray took-off from RAF Lissett at 2230 hours on Friday 2nd June 1944 but, it was destined not to return ... The Reaper's Bomber had been seen over the airfield.

Their target was the marshalling yards at Trappes near Paris and the raid was to commence at 0050 hours on the Saturday morning.

No 158 Squadron supplied 23 bombers for the raid. The total force attacking was 124 bombers and 16 failed to return ... 5 being from 158 Squadron, one of which was X-Xray. Of the seven crew, one was killed, two taken prisoners of war, four evaded capture, one of those being Sergeant Ralph Gilbert who, continued with his poems ... the following is one of them. I trust you enjoy it ...

SPINSTER'S LUCK

Miss Bloggs was a spinster who lived all alone,
In a very large semi-detached,
She had a small cottage near Bournemouth as well,
But this wasn't tiled, it was thatched.

She never had savoured the thrills and delights,
Of hopelessly falling in love,
But at 50 she still hadn't given up hope,
And she prayed to the Lord up above.

Please send me a lover, a great hulking male,
All my treasures I'd trade for a man,
I don't care what shape, or what colour he is,
But make it as quick as you can!

That night in her bedroom, she prayed once again,
And slowly prepared to retire,
To warm up her ardour she had to resort,
To her glowing, wall mounted, gas fire.

She put her false teeth, and her glossy glass eye,
In a jug at the side of the bed,
Then combed the long tresses that hung down her back,
And removed the false wig from her head.

As her eyelashes next she unstuck with some care,
She began to resemble a crock,
With a flick of the wrist, she unscrewed her left leg,
And hung it up under the clock.

And soon she was dreaming of Omar Sharif,
Bob Mitchum, Cary Grant and John Wayne,
And when she had finished, she sighed a big sigh,
And started all over again.

And so she slumbered with mouth open wide,
Emitting a musical snore,
A frightening shadow moved into the room,
As someone sneaked in through the door.

The silent intruder caught sight of Miss Bloggs,
And was almost about to depart,
When he let out a yell, as he stubbed his big toe,
And the spinster awoke with a start.

As she transfixed the robber with one bloodshot eye,
She quickly reached under the bolster,
With a dexterous twist, and a flick of the wrist,
She slid the gun out of its holster.

She looked ugly as sin, and she gave a wry grin,
As the poor fellow stood there and cussed,
He was trembling with fear, as she whispered "Come here".
In a voice that was husky with lust.

"Oh please let me go, I won't do it again",
Said the burglar, who's first name was Greg,
But levelling the pistol, she jumped out of bed,
And stood, standing there on one leg.

"I'm sure you must know, that I can't let you go",
She remarked in a tremulous voice,
"I've been waiting for you, for a decade or two,
I'll be fair though, I'll give you a choice".

"If you'll marry me, then I'll let you go free,
Otherwise mate you are going to get this".
As he viewed her bald head, the last words he said
were "Take aim and make sure you don't miss."

THE PHANTOM BED-CHECKER OF RAF HEREFORD

Each month, on average, I receive about a hundred letters, many with interesting stories and, one such letter was from Jan Thorpe who, encountered some ghostly experiences after she joined the Women's Royal Air Force, the WRAF for short. It all started after she arrived at RAF Hereford for her basic training at the WRAF School of Recruit Training. She ... better still, I will let Jan tell you in her own words about the ... Phantom Bed-Checker of RAF Hereford:

'After having first read two of your Ghost Stations Books, two and four, I felt compelled to write and tell you of my ghostly experiences in the RAF. I joined the WRAF in January 1979 and went to RAF Hereford for my basic recruit training and was billetted in Learoyd block.

'Every evening we were bed-checked at midnight, I think it was. This meant that we all had to be in bed with lights out at this time and, we were checked by the duty NCO who would walk down the full length of the room making sure we were all in.

'The room was occupied by either twelve or fourteen girls, so was quite long. This one particular night the duty NCO was a few minutes early but, as we were all in bed in the dark, we thought no more about it. Until, that is, we were bed-checked again at midnight.

'As I was room leader, I asked the NCO why we were being bed-checked again, was something wrong? She said that this was the first time she had been in and, what was I talking about? There was no way that our 'Phantom Bed-checker' was one of the girls playing tricks as it definitely had metal segs in the shoes and we weren't allowed them until we were due to pass out. Everyone in the room heard it.'

If recruit Jan Thorpe had read Ghost Stations, the first volume and, the story about The Jilted Ghost, she might have had cause to be frightened by the presence of the Phantom Bed-Checker... But now that is gone for in September 1982 the WRAF School of recruit training was transferred from RAF Hereford to form a joint School of Recruit Training at RAF Swinderby in Lincolnshire ... and there, they have their own ghosts!

A GLIMPSE INTO THE PAST

In September 1983 SACW Jan Thorpe was posted to 840 Signals Unit near to RAF Lindholme in Yorkshire. SACW Thorpe's role was telecommunications operator and her Unit was housed in what used to be the Northern Radar buildings. She remained with 840 Signals Unit until June 1986.

In the 1950s we had the 'top secret' ROTOR programme that involved the restoration of 28 wartime above-ground Chain Home stations plus 38 radar stations, 25 in vulnerable areas being underground and the other 13 being semi-underground, all linked by 1,000 miles of new duct line, 3000 miles of cable and, 750 teleprinters. This was the start of the clandestine Gladio Operation. Now the old Northern Radar buildings gave way to new technology and SACW Jan Thorpe takes up the story.

'I was one of the first to be posted in when it became operational but a lot of the lads had been there quite a few months, doing lots of renovations and installing equipment.

'Naturally there were lots of ghost stories and 'queer goings on' stories going round. I must admit that whenever I went upstairs from the traffic hall to the rest room, day or night, I always felt as though someone was watching me as I went up them.

'The only encounter I had with 'time zones' as you describe in your 'Ghost Stations II' was whilst I was at 840 SU. I went over to a filing cabinet in the traffic hall which, was near to the doors which led out to the rest of the building, stairs, offices, police post and entrance and exit turnstile. To go through these doors to the rest of the building you had to go down two steps and the filing cabinet I was standing next to was about six feet away from those steps. The doors had windows in and you had to look down through the windows to see what was going on in the main corridor, though vision was obstructed somewhat by the fact that you were looking down.

'Anyway, this particular day, I was by the filing cabinet and looked through the windows in the door and caught what I've always described as a 'glimpse into the past', as I saw, as plain as day, people walking around wearing old RAF uniforms, what nowadays are known as 'Hairy Mary's.' ... There was a man walking in front of what should have been the turnstile, from right to left as I looked, carrying sheets of paper. Everyone looked very busy. The whole thing lasted about 20 seconds, the time it took me to get something out of the filing cabinet.

A busy wartime airfield - Is this what SACW Jan Thorpe saw..?

'It wasn't until I walked away and thought about what I had seen that I realised it wasn't 'quite right'. I went back to where I had been standing and looked through the windows in the doors and, by the sheer fact that I had to look down to look through the windows and that the turnstile area was about fortyeight feet from where I was standing, I couldn't see the turnstile area at all.

'So I am therefore convinced that I saw a glimpse of the past. Also, at all hours of the day or night we could often smell bacon cooking, even though the kitchen was on the opposite side of the building and even though we knew no-one had been cooking ... A smell from the past, perhaps?'

When I asked Jan Thorpe what sort of feeling she had, she replied: 'I do remember that I felt compelled to look towards the window, almost drawn toward it, if you like, and, that I was aware of no-one else or any other sound around me. It was as if everyone and everything else had disappeared, leaving me alone gazing into the past.' And she added: 'There is no doubt in my mind that I had a privileged glimpse into the past, I know what I saw.'

The traffic hall was always very cold and staff were told that this was due to the air conditioning ... But was there other reasons? Had the supernatural the answer for it being always very cold?

It was certainly more than just the air conditioning. SACW Jan Thorpe said, 'I always felt as though someone was watching me whenever I went up the stairs to the rest room.'

THE GHOST SQUADRONS AT RAF SCAMPTON

As I write, RAF Scampton in Lincolnshire is still an operational airfield but, there are many strong rumours that this once busy wartime airfield will close. And, that is more than likely, seeing that pen-pushers and accountants now rule the Forces. So, it is not security ... but money, that rules and, sadly, the future for RAF Scampton looks very bleak.

So, does that explain why the Ghost Squadrons now take to the skies? To haunt the government's double dealings for shamefully losing faith with those who gave their ALL.

With RAF Scampton still an operational airfield, many who, have heard and, in some cases seen, the Ghost Squadrons, have been too afraid to speak for fear of damaging their RAF careers. And all such cases reported have been covered up. But one not afraid to speak out is Mrs Jan Thorpe.

'In June 1990 my husband was posted to RAF Scampton. I was no longer in the WRAF. We'd heard all the stories of people seeing Nigger and that on certain nights you could hear Lancasters flying.

'This one particular night in October my husband and I were in bed, I was reading and he was fast asleep. When in the distance I heard like a humming, droning noise, that got louder and louder. I was paralysed, not in fear, but in wonder. The noise eventually got overhead and woke my husband up.

As it went directly over our house he jumped out of bed to look out of the window, and there was nothing there at all, just a noise and then it faded away into the distance.

'It was definitely not an aircraft of today and, certainly not one that is at Scampton these days. It wasn't until the next day that we both came to the same conclusion, that it may have been the Lancaster's going off on a mission somewhere.'

Many people at RAF Scampton have reported hearing phantom Lancaster bombers during the month of October and, this could be the Ghost Squadrons taking off and returning from Operation Robinson. This was a dusk raid on the Schneider works at Le Creusot in France and, the two Scampton based squadrons, Numbers 49 and 57, took part. Both squadrons were equipped with the mighty four-engined Lancaster bomber.

Operation Robinson was carried out on 17th October 1942 ... Did Mrs Jan Thorpe and her husband hear the phantom bombers returning ...?

A typical wartime scene ... the Lancaster bombers prepare for take-off.

THE FRIENDLY PHANTOM IN ROOM 15

In March 1991, Brian Stephenson decided to spend a few days in Lincolnshire looking over the old wartime airfields. And, as a Flying Officer in the Volunteer Reserve, he can enjoy the facilities of all Service Messes. He therefore decided to stay at RAF Scampton and was accommodated in Room 15 on the ground floor of the West Wing of the Officers' Mess.

Flying Officer Brian Stephenson arrived at RAF Scampton on Monday 18th March 1991 and, he quickly settled in. He was commissioned in September 1987 and takes great interest in the Royal Air Force, past and present. He was looking forward to the next few days and had come well prepared for all events ... all except a visit by a friendly Phantom, as he now explains:

'It was quite a large room which probably would have housed two people or at least contained quite a bit of furniture; my one small bed, desk and chest of drawers seemed lost in its spaciousness which seemed to amplify the presence of a very large built in wardrobe next to the washbasin - it could have been built into a one time chimney breast judging by the shape of the wall in which it was situated - the wardrobe was not a particularly recent addition judging by its style and dark wood interior, the exterior being white painted.

'On the second evening I opted for a bath before dinner and I duly collected my things and walked a short distance along the corridor to the nearest bathroom. My thoughts were only of my plans for the following morning as I took my bath, in which I lingered longer than intended and I hurried back to my room to dress, not wanting to miss dinner as I was by now quite hungry following my days wanderings.

'My hand was almost on the door handle when I stopped abruptly; I had the strangest but certain feeling that there was someone in my room. Believing that I was about to disturb an intruder I entered the room braced for what I might encounter, but it was quite empty and just as I had left it; I checked around and found nothing out of place but I still felt as though I had been right about feeling a presence.

'After dinner and a couple of beers, I swear it was no more than two, I returned to my room to read for a little while before turning in; no strange feeling this time, I knew my room was alright. I put my trousers and blazer away in the wardrobe and firmly closed the doors which fitted very well and after reading for an hour I turned off my bedside light and fell asleep.

'Something awoke me from a deep sleep, my luminous watch read 03.10 a.m., the wardrobe doors, where my gaze fell as I awoke, were wide open, I thought to myself, half outloud, 'someone has left those bloody doors open again and I'm not getting up to close them'. I knew I did wake, I remember clearly checking my watch, I cannot explain my half spoken exclamation or my annoyance as I rolled over and back to sleep. I again awoke, this time with a start, and this time fully awake, it was breaking daylight and the presence in my room was undeniable, not unfriendly at all or unsettling in anyway, it was almost as though someones departure from the room had awoken me this time, the wardrobe doors were still open. I checked my room door, it was locked, just as I had left it.

'It was still too early to get up and I dozed for perhaps another hour and a half until my radio alarm woke me at seven; Bruce, I swear this is true, the wardrobe doors were now closed, quite firmly too as I had to really tug to open them.

'I stayed another two nights and I really expected an escalation of events but nothing untoward occurred; I felt an unaccountable sadness as I packed my things on the morning of my departure, I felt that I was taking my leave of somewhere that I had known for some time, I spoke a quiet goodbye to the room as I made for the door, or at least that was my belief at the time but, by the time I closed the door seconds later I could not deny that I had addressed the presence that I had felt there and, I somehow understood the sadness I had experienced a little earlier, the kind of sadness known by someone who seems to be destined to be alone.

'It took some time for me to sift my thoughts and come to terms with my feeling, after all, I had come to Lincolnshire in search of the past, I had walked on what remains of R.A.F. Metheringham, I had been to Wellingore and to Coleby Grange, I had found myself in Scopwick churchyard, almost by accident spotting R.A.F. and Luftwaffe graves, yet I had felt absolutely nothing at all when I had been looking for it.

'Incidentally, I discovered your book in Lincoln **after** my experience at Scampton.'

NIGGER ....
THE MYSTERY LIVES ON

Throughout the Ghost Stations Series we have reference to Nigger, Wing Commander Guy Gibson's black Labrador dog and, the mascot of No 617 Dambusters Squadron. Indeed, Mrs Jan Thorpe mentions Nigger in the Ghost Squadrons at RAF Scampton.

But Nigger's death is a mystery and is that the reason why so many people see the ghost dog? It could well be, for the more I thought about it the stranger it became. It does not ring true, and I, as former Royal Air Force Provost Special Security, cannot accept the stories put forward.

We have all seen the 'Dambusters' film where Nigger is seen running around the Station buildings of RAF Scampton looking for his master, Wing Commander Guy Gibson, and, Erks turning the dog away saying, 'No he's not in here.'

Nigger is then seen running from the guardroom - through the **open** main gates and on to the main A15 Lincoln road where a car runs him down.

That is not possible. To be able to run through the **open** main gates. Let me explain, for we are now talking about security - my field.

During the final days of preparation for Operation 'Chastise', the code name for the highly-secret operation, for which, No 617 had been specially formed, RAF Scampton was on maximum security. The Station was sealed. The main gates were **locked** - repeat, **LOCKED.** No one was allowed in or out. No telephone calls could be made. No telegrams could be sent. All leave cancelled. Armed sentries patrolled by the guardroom. This was, of course, usual practise in wartime but, this **was** very special and extra patrols would seal the camp.

And as all dog owners know, a dog has a sixth sense - and Nigger was no exception to the rule. He was an intelligent dog. Gibson was in the final briefing that night - And Nigger would have known exactly where he was. The dog would have sensed that something was 'on' and been very close to his master.

So now we must ask - Why was Nigger left outside?

Why was he not with his batman?

How did Nigger get through the main gates?

And most important - Why should Nigger have wanted to cross the road?

There is only a field, even to this day.

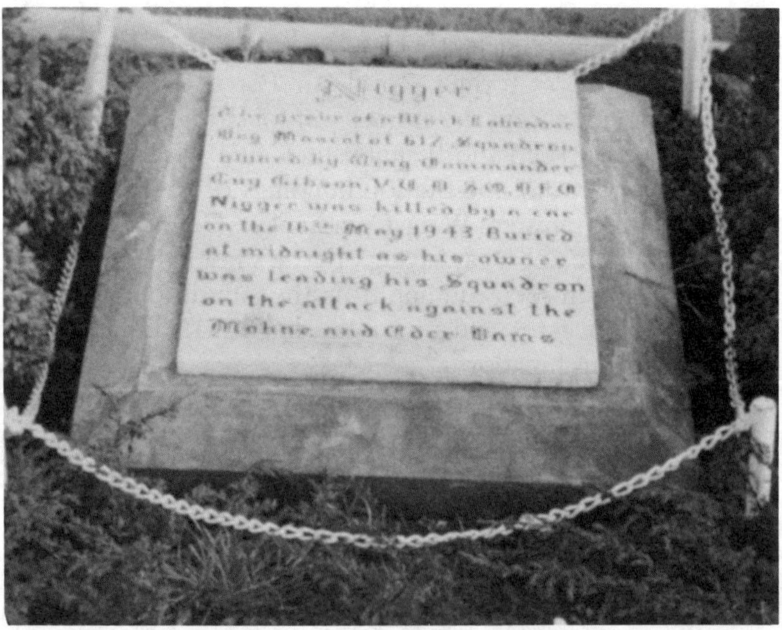

Nigger's grave at RAF Scampton

It was said that the car that ran Nigger down did not even stop. If the gates were sealed - And they were. How did they recover Nigger?

It is all so very strange and I do not believe one word of the original story or, how Nigger is shown to have been killed in the film Dambusters.

No one has mentioned it before - So think about it. There is a cover-up as to how Nigger died.

So what did happen to Nigger?

According to John Sweetman's book, ' The Dam Busters Raid', the driver and passenger of the car were injured in a vain attempt to avoid Nigger. Yet we are told they did not stop!

The more you think about it, the stranger it gets. And, I am certain that you will now ask yourself the same question that I have asked -

How did Nigger really die ...?

THE TRUTH ABOUT LANCASTER R5894 IN DEVIL'S HILL FIELD

The County of Lincolnshire became the last resting place for many aircraft and crew during the second world war. Flying accidents were a daily occurrence and, with the mushrooming of heavy-bomber airfields that sprouted almost overnight in order to meet the demand of Bomber Command, there was a serious problem with overlapping of circuits.

And many crashes were caused by tired crews returning from bombing raids only to find their airfield covered in fog. Battle weary and, battle scarred ... they plunged to earth.

A Lancaster bomber of the type that crashed in Devil's Hill Field

One such doomed bomber was Lancaster R5894. It was trying to land at RAF Scampton in Lincolnshire on Tuesday 2 March 1944 ... but their luck ran out. It was a bad crash and the truth has never been told ... until now.

The official report stated one survivor. But that was not true ... there were no survivors.

Another report said that all crew were killed on impact ... that is not true, as I will prove in a minute.

In Sid Finn's Lincolnshire crash book he states that Lancaster R5894 crashed behind Riseholme Hall ... but that is not true ... it crashed in Devil's Hill Field which, is today haunted by a ghost flyer. And, as the story unfolds, you will understand why it is haunted.

The heavy four-engined Lancaster bomber was on final count-down for landing at RAF Scampton when it hit high tension cables and crashed in Devil's Hill Field, some three hundred yards from the old Roman Ermine Street.

The bomber burst into flames and, with the crash only a short distance from RAF Scampton, the crash rescue teams were quickly on the scene. But, not before the local farmer, Mr Pepper, in whose field the bomber crashed. He was on the scene almost straight away but there was nothing he could do for the aircraft was already burning fiercely ... but he tried ... for the rear-gunner had survived the crash but, was trapped inside his turret.

The only way to get out of the rear-turret was to turn the turret to beam and fall out or, through the doors and into the fuselage ... But both were impossible. The hydraulics out of action. The fuselage a smashed and burning inferno. The rear-turret part lodged in the ground. And on top of that the rear-gunner appeared badly injured. His cries for help fell on helpless ears. In vain, farmer Pepper tried to smash at the rear-turret in a desperate effort to free the badly injured rear-gunner. But all was in vain.

Then the crash rescue team and medical officer arrived from RAF Scampton. By now the bomber was burning fiercely in all sections. The screams continued from the rear-turret and, with great danger to himself, the Medical Officer grabbed an axe from the crash tender and tried in vain to free the trapped rear-gunner. Frantically the Medical Officer hacked at the rear-turret, oblivious to the dangers ... again and again the axe fell as the precious seconds ticked away ... Then, for a split second, the Medical Officer froze ...

Lincs Yeomanry in Riseholme Park and in Devil's Hill Field in May 1909.

Lincs Yeomanry in Egypt - Front row on right as looking at picture - is Percival (Percy) Pepper who had just received his commission.

next second the sharp axe plunged into the rear-gunners head through the smashed turret.

Seeing that all was in vain, the Medical Officer killed the rear-gunner with the axe ... the act being witnessed by farmer Pepper. And, as a former first world war officer, knew that that was the only choice left open to the Medical Officer.

Thus, because of that action taken by the Medical Officer, the reports were made out that all crew were killed on impact and that there were no survivors.

But, there was one survivior ... but he could not be saved and, was killed with an axe by the Medical Officer rather than be left to be burnt alive, for within seconds of that killing deed, the rear-turret was engulfed in flames and a section exploded.

A rear-turret of a bomber and one can see how difficult to get out of.

Today, the high tension cables that the Lancaster bomber hit have been rerouted. When they were brought down, the power supply to Lincoln was cut. The pylon hit was a low pylon in a high spot. On the Ordnance Survey map this section is marked as Tumulus and, marks the true spot where Lancaster R5894 crashed that fateful Tuesday in March 1944 ... And today, it also marks the spot where the ghost flyer haunts in Devil's Hill Field ... and a spine-chilling scream heard on the wind.

John (Jock) Pepper who served in the second world war in the Middle East and Italy with the Indian 8th Army. The son of Percy Pepper who told his son about the Lancaster that crashed in Devil's Hill Field and, how he saw the rear-gunner killed with the axe.

FOUR GRAVES - BUT FIVE NAMES TO SCAMPTON

At 0135 hours on the morning of Monday 12 May 1941 ... just twenty-six hours after the so called Rudolf Hess, the Deputy Fuhrer of Germany parachuted into Scotland ... a German Ju88 was brought down by ground fire from the station defences at RAF Scampton, the kill being credited to Sergeant Walter Billingham - who was later involved with the 'Unseen Servant' at RAF Ossington, Ghost Stations III.

Funeral procession of Leutnant Kurt Hanning and crew of the Ju88 at Scampton village on 14 May 1941. Sergeant Billingham is the one with the shoulder strap to right of the big drum, as looking at the picture. Note: This is a unique photograph being the only known one in existence.

The aircraft crashed in a field where the north-east end of Scampton runway is today. To accommodate the new generation of V-bombers a new runway was laid and, this entailed diverting the old Roman road, the A15, to enable the runway to be extended across the original road.

Four crew members were pulled from the wreckage by a Mr and Mrs Miller of Scampton. All the men were killed and they were buried two days later in Scampton village churchyard. They originally had wooden crosses bearing the names

KURT HANNING (LT)
JOHANNES DIETRICH (GEFR)
WILHELM HANSEN (UFFZ)
E. H. REIDEL (GEFR)

The name Reidel was later changed to read HELMUTH WIMMEDER ...? when the present headstones were added.

A few years later a local farmer, Mr R. Fieldsend, unearthed human remains, including a skull with blond hair attached to it and, bits of aircraft, when ploughing over the site of where the German aircraft crashed.

Very strange ... The Fifth Man. A Ju88 had just enough room for four crew members.

So who was who?

Why was a fifth man on board?

Sergeant Walter Billingam who shot down the German Ju88.

And to add to the mystery the local newspaper, The Echo, reported at the time that a Ju88 was shot down and the entire crew of five perished.

Five crew members? But only four were buried. Why was the fifth crew member not found at the time of the crash?

When the graves in Scampton churchyard were visited by Ken Billingham he said: 'When my dad took me to see the graves in 1963 only four names were seen, no mention of Reidel. When I visited again in 1982, the name E.H. Reidel had been added.'

Very, very strange. The name Reidel had been added with the absence of his date of birth (see photographs). So why did it take so long to sort out the names?

Was it Reidel or, was it Wimmeder on a mission to England?

Was it connected with Rudolf Hess?

To try and solve the mystery, Flight Lieutenant Stockman tried to research the crash and, came up with the findings that a E. H. Reidel went missing at Greifswald, where the Ju88 was based and, was posted as a deserter.

Reidel was never heard of again at Greifswald.

That I do not accept for the following fact based reasons.

The Ju88 which brought Wimmeder and Reidel to Scampton was from 8 Staffel (Squadron) Kampfgeschwader (Bomber Wing) Nr.76, a group which normally operated from bases in France and the Low Countries ... But this aircraft was from Greifswald! A base in north-east Germany about fifty-five miles east of Rostock on the Baltic coast. A very strange airfield to operate from for a routine night raid into Lincolnshire. It would involve a round trip of approximately 1,160 miles - 580 miles each leg of the flight.

So why come all that way when you can do it more easily from either Holland or Belgium?

Four graves ... but five names to Scampton. The four German graves in Scampton Churchyard, the crew of the Ju 88. Note grave top right has TWO names. No date of birth for Reidel.

The reason. It was a Special operation with a Special passenger and, it was connected with Rudolf Hess.

The proof being that the range of the Ju88 A4 which was an improved version of the Ju88 A1/A5 in question, had a range of 1,112 miles, so drop tanks would have to be used - one was reported found in the wreckage!

And the very fact that the drop tank was found in the wreckage proves it very strange. Surely, this would have been used up first and then dumped in the north sea, that was the normal thing to do. Let us remember, one of the so-called Hess's drop tanks was reported found in the River Clyde!

And if Reidel had been a groundcrew chap, I am certain he would not have willingly gone for a ride. So that does not ring true.

To me, it is so very strange and smells like a cover-up.

Just what was going on during those early months of 1941...?

On the night of 20-21 May 1941 a German Dornier, piloted by Oberleutant Schmidt and a crew with M.I.6 connections landed at Lincoln Aerodrome to deliver a package.

Far fetched? But not impossible. It had to be either Waddington or Scampton. Skellingthorpe did not open until October 1941.

So was the incident on 12 May 1941 an operation which went sadly wrong? - Yes. And the FOUR GRAVES - BUT FIVE NAMES TO SCAMPTON bear witness to the cover-up and the mystery.

THE HAUNTED HANGAR AT MIDDLETON ST. GEORGE

During 1987 when RAF Leeming in Yorkshire closed for major redevelopment which, involved building a new control tower, the light aircraft of the University Air Squardon and No 11 Air Experience Flight moved to the old wartime airfield of Middleton St. George - now in business as Tesside International Airport.

Both Units moved into Number 2 Hangar along with one or two other aviation companies who had either equipment or the odd aircraft parked there. Several old offices, long since disused, were quickly pressed into service again and the place seemed to take on a new lease of life.

Lancaster M-Mike landing at Middleton St George just before the end of the war. The haunted hangar is seen on the left.

Wartime crash crew at Middleton St George who knew about the haunted hangar ... it was haunted even then.

The Chipmunk and Bulldog aircraft used the bottom end of the old wartime hangar and, the contracted ground crew Lovaux also had their stores and workshops located there; the washroom for the University Air Squadron and the Air Experience Flight was in the bottom left hand corner ... the haunted section of the hangar as Flying Officer Brian Stephenson explains:

'It was not uncommon to turn expecting to see someone following when crossing the hangar towards the washroom.

'I also noticed a reluctance on behalf of the cadets of the Air Training Corps to use it at all; they would either go in groups or, instead, walk to the airport terminal ... such was their fear for that section of the hangar ... it was very uncanny.

'When I questioned them about it they would simply shrug or, say it didn't feel a very nice place, usually they would reply, 'I don't know, Sir' and appear embarrassed so I never pressed the point with them or mentioned anything said by the staff. It simply wasn't necessary as it was most apparent that everyone shared the same dislike for the place.

'We discovered when clearing out the hangar that badminton courts had been painted on the hangar floor at the bottom end years before and, we quickly acquired a net thinking that the facility maybe useful; but again, no one wanted to use that end of the hangar and would congregate instead at the front door of the hangar whilst waiting for their turn to fly.

'Remember, all these cadets had flown at RAF Leeming in the past and were well used to the hangars and crewrooms, which, were exactly the same ... except for the eerie atmosphere.'

The haunted hangar that Flying Officer Brian Stephenson refers to is infact an old wartime 'J' type hangar and has a long history of being haunted, going back to the war years. In that section of the hangar it has always felt cold and, wartime bombers parked in that area never returned ... and nothing has changed to the present day.

Warrant Officer (later Flying Officer) Brian Stephenson inside the haunted hangar at Middleton St George in March 1991.

During their stay in the old wartime hangar at the old wartime airfield of Middleton St. George the Chipmunks of No 11 Air Experience Flight were continually plagued with faults, usually radio related which baffled the groundcrew.

'For quite a few months, although the radio specialist was of the opinion that the aircraft had been tampered with on occasions his colleagues never went along with his view I always thought they dismissed the possibility too readily, said Flying Officer Stephenson.

Warrant Officer (later Flying Officer) Stephenson inside the haunted hangar with the Chipmunk that was plagued with faults - March 1991.

THE GHOST OF MONTROSE AERODROME

Readers of my Ghost Stations are well aware of The Montrose Ghost and, first told in Ghost Stations with photograph of the funeral of Lieutenant Arthur who, was said to be the ghost of Montrose Aerodrome. And, in Ghost Stations II, More about the Montrose Ghost and, in Ghost Stations III, a full set of photographs showing the military parade and salute over the coffin in the cemetery. And, the caption asks 'But was it an accident...?' If not, that could be the reason why the ghost of Lieutenant Arthur haunts Montrose.

Information now to hand, will help clear up the Montrose mystery, but at the same time give rise to a strange coincidence of two disasters.

Let us go back to the beginning. Lieutenant Desmond Lucius Arthur of the 5th Royal Munster Fusiliers - an Irish Regiment - was born in Glanomere, County Clare, on 31 March 1884. He took his air certificate, No 233, on a Bristol Monoplane at Brooklands on 18 June 1912.

In 1912, Montrose, then a cavalry depot, was handed over to the Royal Flying Club and became the permanent Station of No 2 Squadron. The Squadron were equipped with B.E.2 aeroplanes and, there were many fatal accidents ... mysterious accidents.

One of those fatal unexplained mysterious accidents happened to a pilot named Desmond Arthur in May 1913.

The day he was killed he was flying from the original Montrose Aerodrome at Upper Dysart - about two miles south-west of Montrose - and not from the other flying field at Broomfield which, was one mile north of Montrose. No 2 Squadron moved to Broomfield from Upper Dysart on 15 January 1914, the flying field was then abandoned.

The court of inquiry which sat to investigate the cause of the flying accident found that it was due to an error of judgement on the part of the pilot. But relative and friends of Lieutenant Desmond Arthur were not satisfied with this finding and demanded another inquiry. Another court of inquiry took place, this time under war conditions and, they returned a finding to the effect that the aeroplane had broken up in the air.

Between the two court of inquiries there were many strange happenings and, a strange officer kept appearing at the Officers' Mess and about the Officers' quarters at Montrose. When approached he vanished as suddenly as he had appeared.

Many officers' sighted the ghost airman and, when they reported what they had seen they were taken seriously, for they were officers' and gentleman and, not the sort of people whom one would expect to see things that were not there.

Within the space of only three months dozens reported sighting the ghost. At one time the ghost appeared in the dead of night and stood by the beds of two junior officers who, both saw the ghost very clearly. And such was the publicity, the War Office - as it was then - tried to play down the ghost of Montrose Aerodrome.

At that time, all officers and men in the flying services, had no doubt that the ghost of Montrose Aerodrome was that of Lieutenant Desmond Arthur, haunting the aerodrome in order to get the findings of the court of inquiry on his accident changed. And, because of his numerous appearances and, sinister effect that he had on the whole flying services, there is no doubt, it was the ghost of Montrose Aerodrome that forced the second court of inquiry to change their findings.

The ghost of Lieutenant Desmond Arthur was never seen at the Montrose Broomfield flying field, only at the Officers' Mess which was in an early 19th century army barracks in the centre of Montrose. The body of Desmond Arthur was found near Lunan Bay Railway Station which, is three miles south of Montrose.

A ghost has been seen at Montrose Broomfield but, according to eye witnesses, this phantom figure is clad in second world war flying kit. But there are other eye witness accounts of another phantom figure ... Could this be the spectral Lieutenant Desmond Arthur?

Just after the first world war, Montrose Airfield closed. It re-opened during the expansion period of the 1930s. And, when the ghost was first sighted in November 1940, the Royal Air Force had no doubts that the ghost haunting RAF Montrose was indeed, the ghost of Lieutenant Desmond Arthur. And, on 'arrival chits' issued to those posted to RAF Montrose, it stated that the airfield was haunted by the youngest ghost in the Royal Air Force, an Officer named Flight Lieutenant Arthur.

And could that be so? Yes, for this reason. The Official report on the Lieutenant Arthur hauntings was in a safe at the new Officer's Mess at RAF Montrose. This was the usual wooden building found on all airfields. On the last Friday of October 1940, the building was hit by a German oil bomb. It burned fiercely and the building was destroyed. In the smouldering ashes the safe was opened ... to reveal a pile of ashes ... the remains of the official report. And that is the reason why the ghost of Lieutenant Desmond Arthur returned to haunt the airfield.

THE GHOSTS OF RAF BAWTRY

During the second world war, Bawtry Hall, near Doncaster, became the home for No. 1 group Headquarters. They moved in during July 1941 and by the end of that year was responsible for the bomber airfields at Binbrook, Elsham Wolds, Snaith, Holme, Hemswell and Lindholme. The Group's bombers flew a total of 57,900 operational sorties during the war years, dropping 238,356 tons of bombs and laying 8,147 sea mines. But they paid a high price with the loss of 8,577 aircrew who, perished during Bomber Command's mighty onslaught.

Wartime RAF Bawtry Hall

RESIDENT GHOSTS

Bawtry Hall and the estate was quickly converted into a headquarters for the ever increasing Bomber Command's airfields whose bombers nightly sowed the seeds of death. The boys in blue quickly settled into their spacious operational quarters ... but the wartime guests had not reckoned on the Resident Ghosts ... many airmen reported seeing a White Lady walk across the lake at certain hours of the night. The lake, which was part of the Bawtry Hall estate, was a walk away from the Station proper at the bottom of a ride through woods and, at dusk, with vapour on the water ... it was a very eerie setting ... And it is haunted by the White Lady.

Entrance to RAF Bawtry. As looking at the picture, the building on the left is the old guard-room. The wall on the extreme left was part of the pedestrian way into the MT yard ... the scene of the ghostly foorprints in the snow. The tower of the Hall is visible, left centre. To the right were barracks, cookhouse, playing fields, etc

Bawtry Hall is a three storey building with an impressive frontage, behind which, officers' quarters and mess were situated. In the west wing on the third floor was a 'top secret' office that was locked off from the rest of the building each night. This meant that those on picket duty could not patrol the top floor. The second floor around the courtyard ran all around the building but had only one entrance and exit. It was wood flooring overlaid with lino. Below that were rooms that once served as dairy, stables etcetera and, they were stone flagged floors ... And were also haunted.

One still night all the windows in a billet crashed open in the early hours.

It was a perfectly still night. Not even a breath of wind ... yet all the windows suddenly crashed open ... the building was deserted ... from human beings that is.

There were many other strange and supernatural happenings ... too many for just coincidence. Postcards kept appearing on a mantlepiece on the third floor ... remembering that all material had to be locked away ... which had been left bare the night before. Old postcards which, had come from the back of the fireplace and were slightly charred but not burned.

GHOSTLY FOOTSTEPS

After the second world war the ghostly happenings increased at RAF Bawtry ... it was as if the Spirits of those killed so needlessly ... had come back to haunt those in command.

After his square bashing at RAF Padgate, Aircraftman John Tilmouth was posted to RAF Bawtry for general duties in October 1948. And, seeing that he was a hairdresser in civvy street, he naturally became the Station barber.

Over the Christmas period in 1949 he was on picket duty, armed only with standard issue truncheon and torch. Those on picket duty, were obliged ... because of the area around the 'top secret' office in the west wing being sealed off ... to go around the building to the 'sealed off' west area and, back by the same route.

During his shift, over that Christmas period in fortynine Aircraftman Tilmouth experienced the ghostly footsteps which, is still fresh in his mind after four decades. He recalls:

'As a northerner, I came home for New Year and spent Christmas on the station. As a result I was on picket duty with another chap. One of our duties was to patrol the building described, regularly. It was the day after Boxing Day as I recall and my partner and I went into the building with me carrying the truncheon and the other fellow the torch, we checked the doors. The COs door was in front of us, with the corridor down the west side, at our left. We heard footsteps coming towards us down that corridor and, naturally, shone the torch down the corridor. There was no one there but the footsteps continued. Almost as one man we rushed back to the Duty Officer's room, slammed and locked the door. The footsteps came to the door and stopped. No sound, except from us to push the desk up to the door to prevent entry. We stayed there until dawn, missed our breakfast and, when we finally opened the door, no-one was there. I don't think I ever quite recovered from that. I was terrified and can still feel a little of that now. That is the only incident I personally 'enjoyed'. When it was reported to the Adjutant, it was described as 'Rubbish'. If memory serves, we narrowly escaped being charged. With what, I will never know. As to what became of the truncheon and torch, I do not know.'

Very strange ... but true. Many people who served at RAF Bawtry heard the ghostly footsteps but each time the incidents were reported, they were pooh-poohed at the time but, over the years the stories have emerged.

The post-war years brought peace ... but for many it was a restless peace as the ghost squadrons took over the old abandoned airfields.

GHOSTLY FOOTPRINTS IN THE SNOW

The Crown Hotel in Yorkshire

During the winter of 1949 Flight Lieutenant Shaw was returning to RAF Bawtry after a night out at the Crown Hotel. It was late, and it had been snowing heavily with the ground well covered by a good inch of snow. Shaw, slightly askew with drink, is alleged to have tried to catch the Motor Transport crew sleeping on duty and, had started towards the MT Section when he noticed footprints in the snow ... ghostly footprints appearing beside him as he walked.

The ghostly footprints quickly sobered Flight Lieutenant Shaw, because no-one else was there ... he was alone ... or was he? Had a restless Spirit returned?

Shaw, now stone cold sober, did not wait to find out and he quickly called out the Station police. A search was carried out but no intruders were found ... and no-one could explain the ghostly footprints.

One who witnessed the ghostly footprints in the snow was the Station barber Aircraftman John Tilmouth who, later recalled: 'The footprints commenced at the foot of a wall which was about eight feet high and, there was no disturbance of snow on top. I did see the footprints. I think everyone at RAF Bawtry did. As far as aftermath is concerned, I believe Flight Lieutenant Shaw was posted shortly afterwards and the ghostly footprints in the snow became legend.'

THE HAUNTED PUNCH BALL

One airman stationed at RAF Bawtry had aspirations to be a boxer. He used gym equipment which was kept in the Station recreation hall. That equipment included a punch ball, the type on a tall spring that shoots back when you hit it. But it was much more than just a punch ball, it was a haunted punch ball that moved on its own. No matter where or how it was locked away, it was always found between the two sets of entrance doors, next night.

One of those who witnessed the haunted punch ball was John Tilmouth. 'I can remember once, that he ostentatiously locked everything away in its allotted cupboard, took the key to the Sergeant and left it there,' he said. 'We - three of us - were with him. We went with him next evening to pick up the key, opened the hall and, sure enough, the punch ball was at the entrance doors.'

Today, the Royal Air Force has gone from RAF Bawtry ... but not so the Resident Ghosts and the White Lady walks across the Lake. And in the still of the night ... ghostly footsteps can be heard.

THE DAM BUSTERS CURSE

After intensive training which lasted six weeks, Operation 'Chastise' was launched on 16 May 1943 and the first Lancaster took off before 2130 hours at RAF Scampton.

Nineteen specially modified Lancasters - coded 'AJ' - took part in the raid on the Möhne, Eder and Sorpe dams.

Wing Commander Guy Gibson - centre left, hand in pocket - just after being told to form a special squadron, number 617 Dambusters.

The plan was for Wing Commander Guy Gibson's nine aircraft to attack all three dams, while a diversionary force of five Lancasters attacked the Sorpe and five Lancasters remained in reserve. Dropping their Barnes Wallis spinning mines - nicknamed the bouncing bombs - at 220 miles-per-hour and, at exactly sixty feet, the squadron breached the Möhne and Eder dams. 'Nigger' the code message announcing the success of the operation, was received at St Vincents, Grantham, the headquarters of No 5 Group, Bomber Command.

So much has been said and written about this flight to glory by No 617 Squadron's dams raid. We do know that eleven aircraft out of nineteen got back and fiftythree brave young men died. Guy Gibson lived to fight another day ... But he was cursed for inflicting such terrible damage and slaughter of innocent men, women, children and, animals.

For the first time we now look at the dams raid from the German side and, photographs of the aftermath are shown in this volume for the first time.

From the following, one can get the picture at the Air Raid Warning Centre V1/15 during the night of Monday 17 May 1943, as from 0030 hours. The following is an actual translation of the original Luftschutz - ARWC report.

0030	air raid alarm proposed, sounded at 0031 for Kassel
0034	air raid alarm for south group (Melsungen)
0035	break in the warning net due to battery short-out
0047	Kassel control reported 0045 4 - 6 enemy aircraft at position 82 - target not as yet discernible
0054	Dortmund control reported that at 0051 approx. 8 enemy aircraft circling in areas 823 and 825
0056	Kassel control reported enemy aircraft remaining in 82 on various courses
0100	Momentary report: aircraft activity at 72 and 82

0102	enemy aircraft circling in the Eder Dam area, still no object discernible
0106	Usseln aircraft spotters reported aircraft sounds at 10
0112	Air raid alarm sounded for eastern area report received **that the Möehne Dam had been hit**
0117	and 0118 reports received from aircraft spotters at Winterberg and at Waldeck concerning flares being dropped. The bearings of these reports suggested the Eder reservoir area(!)
0120	power restored to the warning circuit
0130	4 enemy aircraft reported dropping flares over the Eder reservoir
0138	smoke (steam) reported over the dam. Questions also to our unit at the Eder reservoir could, unfortunately, offer no explanation
0149	the dropping of flares continues
0155	further observance of aircraft circling over the Eder reservoir
0205	sounds of aircraft and searchlights over the dam and
0220	the ARP centres at Waldeck and Usseln report aircraft sounds.

When at the Kassel centre it was known that the Mohne reservoir (dam) had been hit. Special attention was paid to the activities of the emeny aircraft in the Eder (Kassel) area.

The continuous circling and the dropping of numerous flares indicated that the Eder dam would be the target this night.

In answer to numerous telephone queries concerning the position from the police, the local government and, the armed forces which were directed to the Air Raid Centre (LSWK) we informed them of the attack on the Möhne dam and the possibility of an attack on the Eder dam.

The Eder dam is breached - Taken 18 May 1943. A photograph no one was allowed to see ... Until now. One can see the vast area breached.

The Eder dam - Taken 19 May 1943. Again no one was allowed to see it. This photograph is the only one known of the west side of the Eder dam and, was taken just two days after breaching. Note that the water level is under the lower edge of the breach. This was due to two pipes of some three metres in diameter, one at each end of the wall, through which water flowed into the turbines of the power stations.

The air situation was correctly interpreted as well as the importance of the (Eder) dam to the Kassel area and the city of Kassel. The wide-ranging consequences in the event of damage to the dam and the resulting flooding.

0201	0200	82683	(Usseln) aircraft noise low at 6-8
0202	0200	82811	(Winterberg) aircraft noise high at 3-1
0204	0203	92711	(Waldeck) 4 enemy aircraft- 4--engined retreating direction 9
	0202	82683	(Usseln) aircraft noise low 4-7
0205	0201	82311	(Beckum) aircraft noise low 9-10
	0205	92711	(Waldeck) 4-engined aircraft noise light beams over dam
0206	0206	Hs	(Henschel) Altenbauna in area 9 nothing to see (report)
	0204	82724	(Fredeburg) aircraft noise high area 11
	0204	82761	(Oberkirchen) aircraft noise high at 1-12
0207	**Periodic report 19: aircraft 'lingering' in Marsberg - Reservoir area**		
0208	0206	82451	(Oberntudorf) aircraft noise low at 3
0213	0208	82374	(Korbecke) 1 enemy aircraft 4-engined low at 4-10
0216	0215	82374	(Korbecke) aircraft noise high at 6-4
0218	**Periodic report 20: aircraft from the Eder reservoir** area retreating to NW		
	0213	82353	(Wiegeringhausen) aircraft noise low 10-11, distant high (!)
0223	0220	82683	(Usseln) aircraft noise medium height at 3, distant high
0225	0224	82663	(Rosenbeck) aircraft noise at 7
0226	0215	92711	(Waldeck) aircraft noise high at 9, distant high

0227 0222 82311 (Beckum) continuous aircraft noise medium height at 12-11

0229 0227 82874 (Battenberg) aircraft noise high at 3-2, distant high

0235 **Periodic report 21: One enemy aircraft circling in area Marburg/Lahn**

0236 **ADVICE FROM BAD WILDUNGEN.THE CENTRE AT MAUSER FACTORY AT WALDECK REPORTS 'AFFOLDERN IS UNDER WATER (FLOODED), HOUSES COLLAPSING.'**

0242 Periodic report 22: THE EDER DAM HAS BEEN HIT

0258 Periodic report 23: 3 aircraft circling in area Dortmund-Munster various courses

0300 All clear given for Witzenhausen-Eschwege

0301 All clear given for railway group east

0308 **Air raid warning lifted for Kassel**

0311 Air raid warning for railway groups central and south lifted

0312 All clear given for Melsungen

0314 Periodic report 24: The air situation in our area has quietened down, west of Arnsberg-Munster little enemy activity

Note...

It is interesting to see that the Air Raid Warning Control Centre in Kassel which, made this report, did not receive the advice that the EDER DAM had been hit until 0242. At 0236 they received a report from the Mauser factory at Waldeck which, is at the Eder reservoir, that Affoldern was under water. This village is on the bank of the Eder river 4 kilometres down-stream. At 0218 Periodic report 20 states, 'enemy aircraft retreating to NW'.

Possibly the centre did not believe the report of 0236 and 0242!

As the drama unfolded in the night sky above them, the residents of the nearby village of Affoldern took to the adjacent hills in order to escape the approaching death flood.

Under the command of Wing Commander Guy Gibson the bombers were circling in preparation for an attack against the unprotected Eder dam.

Time and again the lead bomber circled the area around the dam, as if willing his bombers to create mass destruction ... This was Gibson's Lancaster and, it was picked-out by a young German housewife who, was one of the lucky ones that managed to find high ground before the dam burst.

She followed the deadly silhouette of Gibson's bomber ... and shivering with fright she uttered, 'Curse you, you evil Terror-Flieger, curse you. I, Frau Kloppman, curse you, lead Terror-Flieger, to crash and die a horrid death by fire, for you, are from the Teufel.'

She was frightened. She was mad. And quite rightly so. The night of 17 May was a nightmare for at that stage of the

Eder dam taken two days after breaching. And no one was allowed to see it. In foreground is a power station and another one far left adjacent to the dam wall. Some construction equipment can be seen on top of the dam wall behind the flagpole.

The devastion. Kassel on 19 May 1943... thousands killed and missing. Another rare photograph shown here for the first time.

war, the German people were already poor and hungry. Now, what food and animals they had, had been destroyed in the death flood.

Hundreds of people experienced the nightmare wall of water that washed away their houses and property under the Eder dam - the type of house in this area being 'Tudor' style, substantial beams filled in with straw and plaster.

The day after the dams raid, Frau Kloppman's husband, Heinrich, came on leave to his home at Dornberg. At great risk to their lives, Heinrich Kloppman and his wife cycled to a spot, protected by bushes, overlooking the dam via Ippinghausen, Sachsenhausen and Werpe, some 35 kilometres. Here they took photographs using a Kodak 6 x 9mm camera.

They took a great risk taking the photographs for it was forbidden to take any photographs. And, at this period there were many guards at all key points. But that did not stop

Kloppman taking two sensational photographs - as we can now see.

It did help with Kloppman being in his Panzer uniform. And, the vast destruction, also helped, for the Flak Units had to detour via Dornberg due to the approach roads being washed away. The Kloppman's gave some schoolboys 50 pfennig for helping to carry their bicycles over the obstacles.

From the top of a hill they were able to see Affoldern which, was flooded.

Then came the difficult task in getting the film developed. A Kassel photographer refused outright to develop and print the film and quickly turned them away.

After Heinrich Kloppman had gone back to his unit, the 1st Panzer Division which, was then in occupied France, Frau Kloppman gave the film to a friend who in turn, took it to another friend who, worked at the IG Farben factory at Hoechst, near to Darmstadt. Relatives then brought the unique photographs and the negatives back to Frau Kloppman who, immediately hid them away.

The official documents state that the raid on the Ruhr dams led to 1,294 deaths and that most of these were near the Mohne dam, especially in the town of Neheim-Husten that suffered over 900. All were drowned. But unofficial figures say well over 5,000 were killed. There is no record of animal casualties for they were vast.

Meanwhile, the curse and the photographs remained Frau Kloppman's secret.

Back in England, Frau Kloppman's curse was starting to work ... saving Gibson for his special curse, for he was from the Teufel, the Devil ... Thirty-five of the Dam Busters were killed in three nights within a month of Gibson being posted to 'special duties' in August 1943.

The raid against the Ruhr dams had been a costly failure. Yes, the damage to power stations, factory buildings, houses, roads, bridges and to agriculture was enormous and wiped out complete families. But it was only done to smash the will of

Back at RAF Scampton, the King bends over the target photographs while Gibson looks on ... unbeknown that a curse had been cast.

the German people, for Bomber Command made no attempt to stop the repair work on the dams.

So Frau Kloppman was right to curse the Terror-Fliegers for the dam raid was political. But it earned Gibson the Victoria Cross.

On the night of 19-20 September 1944 Wing Commander Guy Gibson volunteered to act as Master Bomber and, set course in his borrowed de Havilland Mosquito for Rheydt, just inside the German border.

Gibson left the target area ... but the curse was now to be played out. According to eyewitnesses, Gibson's Mosquito was seen to crash in flames near the town of Steenbergen-en-Kruisland in Holland.

A ball of flame ... just as the curse stated. And for many years, the crash was not identified ... forgotten.

In early 1987, Frau Kloppman let the sensational photographs, that she and her husband took in May 1943, see the light of day and, I was first to have a copy and, the documents with the photographs.

Now that the photographs have come to light and, the curse on those Terror-Fliegers that launched the death flood on so many innocent men, women, children and animals, also made known, it does help to explain the mystery around Wing Commander Guy Gibson's death ... 'seen to crash to the ground in a ball of flame,' said eye witnessed accounts of Gibson's crash ... consumed by fire!

THE EDER DAM MYSTERY

'Get a message out to Group,' cried Gibson to his radio operator.

'Nigger! Nigger! Nigger!'

Nigger was the code word for the breaching of the Mohne dam. Gibson's job was now done. Gathering the rest of the formation, he headed for the Eder dam but when he got there they found that mist had developed and it made it difficult to get a clear run. The one consolation being no flak.

Flight Lieutenant Dave Shannon attacked first but after five unsuccessful runs withdrew to get a fresh look at the target. Squadron Leader Henry Maudsley, flying Lancaster AJ-Z-Zebra, made the next run but the 'bouncing bomb' was released too late and it exploded on the crown of the dam, doing very little damage but destroying the bomber in a blinding flash.

The Eder dam - August 1943.....Then

Or did it ...? On his third run in Gibson reported seeing something hanging below Z-Zebra, thought to be damaged. Gibson and others saw Maudsley's 'bouncing bomb' drop too late and explode on impact with the dam parapet.

And now the mystery. Gibson's crew were adamant that Z-Zebra was beyond the explosion - not above it.

And the mystery deepens. Gibson called-up Maudsley and on the second call a 'faint' voice was heard to say, 'I...think...so...stand...by'.

Sergeant O'Brien thought that the very faint sound was unnatural and almost de-humanized. But it was definately heard.

The official verdict was that Squadron Leader Maudsley had been blown up by his own mine. But later evidence supports the conclusion that Maudsley did in fact survive.

And at this point the mystery now becomes sinister. German records on this operation have not survived. British casualty records are not open to public inspection. It is therefore impossible to conclude that Maudsley did survive with any certainty.

The Eder dam - August 1989 ... Now.

YET ANOTHER ... LAVENHAM EXPERIENCE

It all started with a visit to the museum at the old East Kirkby bomber airfield in Lincolnshire. After being shown the collection of books on sale in the souvenir shop, Lance Tebbutt purchased a copy of my Ghost Stations, the first volume.

'With a copy of Ghost Stations which, I read cover to cover, my hobby number two started,' said Lance Tebbutt, aged 29.

Lance Tebbutt - as looking at the picture the one on the left - and his friend

In September 1984 Lance Tebbutt came out of the Royal Air Force after serving six years as an RAF crash rescue fireman. 'I joined the Royal Air Force on leaving school,' he said. 'Whilst I was serving I just took the RAF as a job and didn't really take any interest in flying or the airfields. The only hobby I really took to was my love of motor-bikes and the history of the RMS Titanic which has been a study-come book and memorabilia collection.'

Born at Sleaford in Lincolnshire, in what is called bomber county, Lance soon became interested in the old airfields and, also, the airfields of the American Eighth Air Force, as he now explains:

'I decided that I would like to make and experience my own collection of old airfields of the Eighth and U.K. Stations on colour slides from my camera. So my friend Gary Clarke and, myself, started going round East Anglia on my new motor-bike armed with camera and books; eventually we ended up at the old wartime Station of Lavenham, number 137.

'We obtained permission from one of the local farmers a Mr Eady, to take a look around the old tower ... keeper of memories and, the airfield. Quite a lot of Lavenham still remains and after shinning up the old tower ... which was glazed and locked-up ... for a good look inside, we were approached by a car, so I quickly jumped down from the balcony of the tower.

'The driver of the car turned out to be Mr Eady's brother ... also a farmer on the land ... accompanied by his wife and their dog.'

Lance and Gary introduced themselves and at the same time informed them that they had obtained permission from his brother. Mr Eady told them that the control tower had been lived in by an old game-keeper just after the Americans departed in 1945. He then unlocked the tower and invited Lance and Gary to look around inside. They jumped at the offer.

'It was during our look inside the tower that Gary and myself had our own Lavenham Experience,' said Lance.

For those who are not Ghost Stations Fans, the Lavenham Experience that Lance Tebbutt refers to is the story of June Constable and her friend Philippa who, after getting lost, ended up on the old airfield at Lavenham and, is told in my Ghost Stations. Their story is called The Lavenham Experience and, it is this story that Lance Tebbutt refers to.

Lance Tebbutt continues: 'We stood in the top floor of the tower with Mr and Mrs Eady and their dog, looking at the old Flight blackboard and admiring the condition of the old parquet flooring.

'As we were looking at the floor, Mr Eady decided to check that all the windows were secure and, after adjusting the latch on one of the windows that didn't want to close properly, it was at that point we heard this strange eerie sound. True enough the wind seemed to pick-up and Gary said, 'Listen!' At that very moment Mr Eady's dog shot out of the tower, followed by Mr Eady to retrieve him ... sure enough ... born on the wind through that window we could clearly hear the noise of heavy-bombers flying over the airfield. It was absolutely chilling to us yet at the same time, very exciting.

'By this time Mrs Eady had walked out of the room, leaving me and Gary transfixed to the floor and window. Our Lavenham Experience lasted about forty-five seconds. We were utterly amazed, that on leaving the control tower, it was a beautiful ... still, summer evening, not a hint of wind. I remember it very clearly for we had a smoke once outside and our cigarette smoke went straight up. No wind, not even a breeze,'

So two more had the Lavenham Experience and, when Lance and Gary asked Mrs Eady if she had heard the noise, she replied that she had heard a sort of sound like aeroplanes passing overhead. Was that why the dog bolted from the tower ...?

I must just add that Lance Tebbutt has asked me to make it very clear that neither he, nor his friend Gary, are ghost busters or trivia seekers. And, I must stress this point.

The American crew of 'You Cawn't Miss it' pose by their bomber.

'The reason for telling the story is because, of all the Eighth Airfields and RAF Stations, that we have visited, we have neither looked for, or experienced, anything at all.' said Lance Tebbutt. 'Apart from the old airfield at Lavenham.'

An American Boeing B-17, bomb doors open, starts its bombing run under a murderous hail of flak ... Did it make it back to Lavenham ...?

Their visit to the old airfield at Lavenham took place during the first Sunday in August 1991 at approximately 1930 hours.

'After we all said our goodbye's to each other, Mr and Mrs Eady and their little dog, drove off,' said Lance. 'Gary and myself then stood back and looked at the old control tower. We both seemed to feel a sense of triumph ... as if we had been cheering the bomber's on.' And he added. 'This was a very, very real experience and I feel quite sure it was not my imagination running away with itself.'

No, it was not his imagination for it affected them all in the tower ... even the little dog. It was certainly another ... Lavenham Experience.

The control tower at Lavenham visited by Lance Tebbutt and his friend. As you look at the picture it was the top window on the right where they experienced the ghosts of yesteryear.

A CHILLING EXPERIENCE AT EAST KIRKBY

And following yet Another ... Lavenham Experience, we have the chilling experience at the old East Kirkby airfield. The next story shows how each airfield weaves its own mystical spell ... in many different ways. To many they are just old airfields ... but to others they have feeling ... a spell-like magic that draws you to stop and ponder awhile. There is a tear on the wind as you pass the abandoned airfields that refuse to fade away.

Lancaster NX 611 seen here outside RAF Scampton but now at East Kirkby.

'I read with great interest your book Ghost Stations as I have always been interested in flying, especially with the second world war,' said Graeme Garnham. 'We, my wife Janice and I, often take our caravan to the Lincoln area which, we both like and occassionally look around derelict air stations. After reading your book we had a twilight wander on the runways and taxiways at Fiskerton, but no jeep appeared!

'I have been told I am susceptible to unusual atmospheres, and often fancy I sense something which sets the hairs on my neck up, but Janice doesn't sense this the same as I do. A couple of years ago we were exploring Lincolnshire, with our caravan based at Cherry Willingham, just outside Fiskerton. We'd gone to see the excellent display of the Battle of Britain Memorial Flight at Coningsby and really enjoyed ourselves. From there we decided to go over to East Kirkby museum. This being Easter 1989, the museum hadn't had the Scampton Lancaster long, and we had a good look around the hangar. The control tower had been restored so this is where we went next. Janice enjoys wandering around slowly, while I tend to take things in much quicker, so we looked around downstairs first then I went up to the observation floor, followed by my wife a little later. It was while I was up there that I began to get a chilly feeling of not being alone. Janice was in the corridor reading some framed accounts of RAF V.C.'s when I went into a room displaying flying equipment and a WAAFs uniform on a tailor's dummy. This room was the first on the right at the top of the stairs.

'I took a glance in, but the atmosphere was one of chill. I was definitely not alone, and didn't stay but went out into the corridor to tell Janice I was going outside. She agreed to come with me, this was unusual, as she generally likes to see everything in her own time and won't be hurried, so she left without seeing much of the upper floor, apart from the corridor with its framed V.C.'s.

'When we got outside we stopped and chatted - I told her how and what I had felt, and she surprised me by saying that the reason she had been reading aloud was that she had felt someone was reading over her shoulder, and she read aloud through fear! As I said before she doesn't usually respond to atmospheres, but this time we both felt as if we didn't want to stay there, that we weren't alone in the tower. The feeling was chilling, but not malevolent or dangerous, just ... there.'

The old RAF East Kirkby Airfield was home to Nos 57, 460 and 630 Squadrons during the war years. After the war, it housed a detachment from 139 Squadron and, from August 1954 until 1958 the airfield was used by the United States Air Force who deployed a few Dakotas to this once busy bomber airfield. It closed in 1958 and, today, the control tower, Type 12779/41 (see photograph on page 81 of my Ghost Station II) is now restored (with ghost) and the airfield is now known as the Lincolnshire Aviation Heritage Centre that preserves... visual and spiritual memorabilia ... from the war years.

THE SKELLINGTHORPE EXPERIENCE

And another to fall under the mystic spell of the old wartime airfields is James Silver, who wrote to me on Tuesday 5th of May 1992, after his eerie experience at the old Skellingthorpe airfield, on the outskirts of Lincoln ... Just like Lance Tebbutt and his friend, James Silver had an experience ... this then, is his experience, in his own words, he recounts his unexpected and strange Skellingthorpe experience:

The old RAF Skellingthorpe control tower, as in 1967. Now all is gone and only the Spirits of yesteryear remain to haunt the old airfield.

"Yesterday, being Bank Holiday, I decided to cover a little bit more ground and the target was to visit Fiskerton. When I looked at the map, the name that stood out of the page at me was not Fiskerton, but Skellingthorpe. I am sure that this was coincidence, but I must tell you that it was quite clearly the first place that I saw when I opened the map book.

'I had decided to visit at tea time/early evening for the twin reasons that it would be less busy on the roads and for the slightly more personal reason that I have found greater satisfaction from choosing early evening as there is something more 'alive' about these places at that time. Before I go any further I would like to say that I am not a psychic and neither am I a sceptic, I like to keep a totally open mind on all things, believing that there is more to heaven and earth than most can see and all opinions and experiences should be respected. I am now going to tell you exactly what happened to me at Skellingthorpe yesterday.

'I arrived in Skellingthorpe village at a little after 6.30 p.m. I could find nothing except the old railway line and decided to stop and ask a man who was doing the gardening outside his house. He re-directed me over to the other side of the dual carriageway and down a road next to a petrol station, I think it is called Birchwood Avenue. I stopped again and asked a teenager where the old bomber station was and he told me that it was now a housing estate but if I took the third turning on the left, that is where it used to be. I followed his instructions and drove down that road, seeing the new houses on the right at the bottom. I could see no signs of any vestige of an airfield. I saw a man walking on the pavement so I wound down the window and asked him the whereabouts of the airfield. He told me that there was no remnant of it but there was a monument and if I went back up the road and turned left it would be on my left. I asked again if there was any sign of buildings or airstrip. He was by now leaning in through the window and was watching me carefully. His immediate answer to the question was no and he continued to watch me. I asked again if he was sure and he then asked to get in the car and he would show me. He was already in by the time I had said 'o.k.' He told me to turn around and we went back up the road about three hundred yards before he told me to stop and get out of the car. He then said 'it is here', and walked over a mound of what looked like grass on the left of the road but it was actually rubble. On the other side of this rubble bank there is a football field and also about two hundred yards of runway. On the right of the runway there are piles of rubble that are presumably the ruins of the station buildings. What follows is recounted to you in as straightforward a manner as I can manage. You must also remember that this was a warm Spring evening and there is no wind to speak of. It was still daylight.

'The moment I stepped on the runway it became icy cold. There was a wind blowing straight in my face. My chest went tight and I could feel my heart was pounding. The man who had shown me the runway turned round and asked me if I could feel anything. I did not tell him what had happened to me but I did say that I could and that it had gone very cold. He just nodded and then he set off up the runway. When I started walking I could not feel my legs. I do not know how I got moving. We walked all the way up the remaining runway and turned right to the monument, which is at the edge of a social club car park. It is a well designed and thoughtful tribute and within the square of the monument area the temperature returned to normal. The man who was with me was about to tell me something that had happened to him but he kept refusing to say more when I asked him further. He did say that he now felt cold which I thought strange as it was so much warmer in that little square of the memorial. He intoduced himself as Barney. He shook my hand and his hand was icy cold. He had had his hands in his jacket pockets all the time. He asked me if I wanted a drink in the social club and I said no, because I was driving. He then said that he must go and I thanked him for his help. I did not see him after he walked out of the perimeter of the memorial area. When I stepped out of the area to film the memorial, the same cold feeling returned and continued until someone said 'Is this all there is?' This startled me and I turned and saw a man with a stills camera. I told him that there was also some runway and building rubble at the back of the monument and he photographed the monument and then went to look at the runway. I did notice that the coldness and other feelings had gone and these did not return until I walked back onto the runway. They were also present, to a lesser extent, while I was walking over the piles of rubble. When I left the runway and returned to the car everything was as it had been before I started. I cannot guarantee this but I am fairly certain that there was no noise from the surrounding area while I was on the runway, despite there being people on the football pitch, traffic noise etc. There is also my video recording, which makes interesting listening/watching.

'What I must say is that the feelings were not fear. I did not feel frightened. The best way I can describe this is as some sort of excitement or anticipation as if some great event were about to take place, and I was becoming part of it. Maybe that was the event or maybe, had someone else been there with a trained mind or more experience than me, they could have made more of what I can only describe as a massive force of will centred upon that short strip of runway and, to a lesser degree, in the rubble of the airfield buildings. I have put down the parts of this experience that are most directly related, but I must ask if there was ever a member of the RAF killed on that airfield while he was off duty (or possibly a civilian). If you can answer this, it may explain some more of the events of yesterday.

'What I have told you is a factual, truthful account of the events, put down in the best way I can think of to describe them.'

James Silver asks if any airman or, civilian, were killed on Skellingthorpe Airfield. The answer is yes on both accounts. On that short strip of runway ... or should I say beneath it, for it happened before construction of runways proper ... to which he refers, a twin-engined Manchester bomber blew-up on take-off killing all crew members.

No 50 Squadron converted to the fateful Manchester in April 1942 and there was always tight security around the troublesome bomber. There were many crashes and the aircraft easily caught fire. Only half of the Manchester bombers were operational at any given time and, they caused many a loss of life. For that reason reports and crashes were covered up, such was the fear of those in command. But some good came out of the terrible accidents for from the twin-engined Manchester came the four-engined Lancaster.

And was a civilian killed? There was a very strange incident that was surrounded in secrecy regarding a man in civvies who, was killed along with all the crew members when their bomber crashed on take-off. Whether this was a civilian or, a member of the RAF in civilian clothes, I do not know. I do know that the cloak of secrecy covered the incident. And that could part answer the Skellingthorpe Experience.

THE 'GLOWING' CONTROL TOWER

Between 1986 and 1988, David Peel lived at RAF Hemswell, in the Post Office on the Market Rasen road. The Post Office served the army camp that occupied part of the old airfield.

In February 1987 he was at a loose end one night and, half seriously, suggested to his brother and his best friend, that they should go on a ghost hunt at the airfield opposite ... the old RAF Hemswell.

The three of them set out and after exploring almost the entire airfield ... when suddenly, David Peel halted: 'I noticed what I thought was a greenish 'glow' at the top window in the control tower,' he said. 'After the 'you are seeing things' and rubbishing me, it was agreed that there was some sort of green light inside the top room in the tower.

'Rather excitedly we managed, possibly illegally, to get on to the roof .. trying to 'hang off' the railings in order to get a look into the window that was 'glowing' but, sadly we were not able to.

'Probably nothing at all in it but, I did lay awake for a long time that night just wondering what, if anything, we had seen. It was a funny feeling ... I can assure you.'

There have been many ghostly happenings at the old Hemswell airfield, as Readers of my Ghost Stations are well aware. When Derek Harrison - the Missouri Waltz story page 34 in Ghost Stations - paused that October night in 1978 to answer a call of nature in the hedge bordering Hemswell airfield, the last thing in the world he expected to hear was music, voices and, the sound of a piston-engined aeroplane starting its engines ... The airfield was in total darkness and deserted ... or was it?

When I asked David Peel for permission to publish his story, he replied: 'You may certainly use the story if you wish, although it should be stressed that we never actually saw anything tangible or concrete. We only went on the ghost hunt for something to do on a dark night, we never expected to see or hear anything out of the ordinary and, although I cannot explain the 'glow' that definitely came from inside the tower, I wouldn't immediately come to the conclusion that something spectral was afoot at Hemswell, simply on the basis of my experience, although your books would seem to indicate that something is going on at Hemswell RAF.'

THE PHANTOM FOOTPRINTS AT DANESFIELD HOUSE

During the war years Phantom Footprints suddenly appeared on the celling of the great hall at Danesfield House that had been taken over by the Royal Air Force. No one could explain the Phantom Footprints. At many RAF Officers' Messes there could usually be found a footprint on the ceiling, usually put there after a particularly convivial evening.

But the Phantom Footprints at Danesfield was not a practical joke ... it was too sinister to be a joke.

After the war RAF Danesfield was occupied by No 90 Signals Group and when this Unit (then Signals Command), closed in the mid-1970s, the house and buildings on the south side of the road were empty for a long time. Eventually the barrack blocks, NAAFI, domestic site and sports field were taken over by the MoD Police as a training centre and area headquarters.

Danesfield House and its 65 acres proved very difficult to sell. Eventually it was bought by Carnation Foods who spent over a million pounds refurbishing the house. But, after Nestle took over Carnation Foods the house and estate was put up for sale. It was eventually bought by a Swedish company who planned to convert Danesfield House into a luxury hotel.

The work soon got underway, no expense being spared. Company carpenters workshop was brought on site to repair all the carved woodwork and, a large plaster works was installed with skilled workmen to replace and repair the plaster ceilings.

All was going well ... Or was it? Just before the work was completed, a workman saw the Phantom Footprints. He said it was a warning. A few weeks before the planned opening a fire started in the roof timbers above the minstrels gallery in the great hall ... just above the ceiling area where the Phantom Footprints appeared.

The fire destroyed the whole of the interior and part of the courtyard but, not the tower or the stables.

The cause of the fire was unknown. It was suggested that it might have been started by a workman's blowlamp for men were working on the lead on the roof. But those who saw the Phantom Footprints know otherwise.

But the owners were not discourged and, work once again, got underway to refurbish Danesfield House. Nothing could stop them this time ... Or could it? The ceiling in the great hall had perished in the fire and, with it, the Phantom Footprints ... Or had they?

Once again, Danesfield House was brought back to its former glory ... and once again ... the Phantom Footprints appeared on the new ceiling in the great hall. Why did they appear? No one knows or, if they do, they are not saying.

Within a few weeks of the planned opening the building again caught fire. Again the sighting of the Phantom Footprints had heralded a fire.

Once again the owners set to work to rebuild Danesfield House ... the building haunted by the Phantom Footprints.

Danesfield House is at the time of writing again rebuilt and everything is in order ... Or is it? That depends on the Phantom Footprints ... to date they have not reappeared!

THE GHOSTS OF THE SOUTH CHINA SEAS

After the second world war Captain (later Major) Robert Keith Jones was with a War Graves Unit serving with War Crimes Investigation. 'I had, or met, several odd occurrences with first hand knowledge which, I can only describe as supernatural,' he said. 'There can be no doubt that some force occassionally manifests itself which, the layman either rejects, or, accepts as the supernatural.'

Captain Robert Keith Jones in Western Sumatra.

Major Jones has been all over the Far East, following Service in Burma and, is one of the very few who have been all over Java, Sumatra, Malaya, Burma, the 'Death Railway', and most of the lands and islands in the South China Seas looking for evidence of war crimes. He explains:

'I should explain that the job entailed a vast amount of investigation as to how soldiers and civilians had met their death during the Japanese occupation of the Far East. As many as possible were exhumed from their far flung graves and reinterred in the massive cemetary at Singapore and, if some were found to be buried with their hands tied behind their backs they had obviously not died from natural causes.

Chinese prisoners being buried alive by the despicable Japanese.

'During this particular incident in 1946 I was based at Singapore; I was provided with a 61 foot RASC motor launch, capable of about 8 knots maximum speed, with an army crew of four men - the skipper being a Corporal. My instructions were to investigate some burials on various Islands south of Singapore and, as far south as the Sunda Straits - between Java and Sumatra. In fact, on this particular occasion, I landed on every one of the Islands in the Rhio and Linga Archipelago. The sea was like a millpond for the whole month of my stay afloat, the sun was high and bright every day and, nothing happened which was in any way out of the ordinary. Besides the crew of four, my party consisted of myself in charge of the operation, a Staff Sergeant and four British Other Ranks, all of whom were trained soldiers who had been

The despicable Japanese. This picture shows Japanese army recruits being instructed in the use of the bayonet with prisoners as targets.

More human targets for Japanese soldiers. This photograph was smuggled out of Shanghai. Plenty of proof for Captain Jones ... but they were never made to pay for their despicable war crimes.

through the war in Burma, were intelligent men and, amenable to discipline.

'A specific task was to find and recover the remains of an Australian Nurse and Doctor suspected of being murdered by the Japanese in 1941. I had been given the names of the victims and the Island on which they were buried and, they were quickly dubbed Frankie and Johnny by the crew. The bodies were recovered, or what few bones remained of them, each was wrapped in a blanket, tied with wire, labelled and, placed one on each bow seat of the launch, protected by the bow but, otherwise open to the sky. They had been buried side by side on the Island with Frankie on the left and Johnny on the right, according to which end of the graves they were viewed but, such was their state of decomposition it was impossible to tell which was which. They were placed in the same relative positions on the bow seats, in distinctive blankets, so that even had the labels been washed off, or the remains dislodged during heavy seas - which one normally expects in the South China Seas - we would know which was which. Further, the crew and, my own men, were given strict orders that the bow position of the launch was out of bounds except in an emergency and on the orders of the Skipper. And, to make it very clear, I then drew a white line across the deck, six feet back from the bows, so that all on board knew

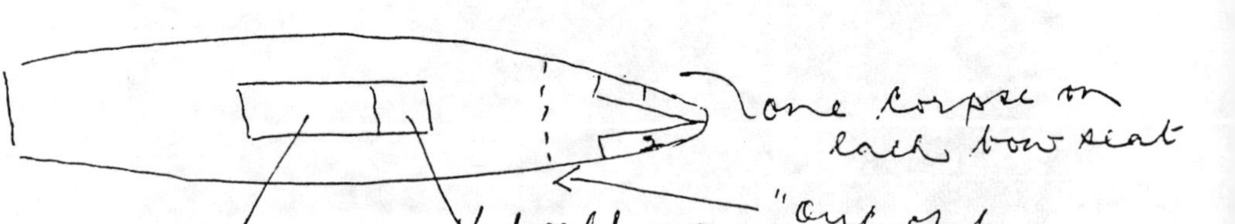

Drawing of the boat by Captain Jones to show position of corpse on the bow seats. Note. The steel wire used to tie the corpse was field cable.

the area that was 'out of bounds'. We then started back to Singapore.

'The following morning the position of the blankets containing the remains were reversed, i.e., Frankie was on the right and Johnny on the left. I returned them to the original position, called the men together and told them that I was displeased that my order had not been obeyed. All assured me that no-one had been near the bows and, the Skipper added two points - 1) that sailors were superstitious and would not go near dead bodies anyway - in fact my own men had to do all the handling - and, 2) that he had been on the bridge all night, that it had been bright moonlight all the time, that the bow of the launch had been in full view of the wheelhouse all the time and, that no-one on board had been further forward than the bridge (amidships).

'Nothing happened all that day but, the following morning the position of the remains had again been reversed. Once again, I returned the remains to their original position, called the men together and, expressed in strong terms that I considered someone was playing a joke, that I did not see the funny side and, left them in no doubt as to what would happen if they did it again. I was nevertheless assured that nobody had been near the bows. Their protestations were so strong, not to say indignant, that I discussed the matter at some length with my Staff Sergeant and, we decided to remain on watch together all that night. We both accepted the fact that the crew were not to blame and, that our own men would not play such a practical joke in contravention of a direct military order. I may add that the relationships between everyone on board, including myself, were most cordial and, there was no alcohol consumed while sailing. What little canned beer we had was locked up at sea. We were on the return trip to Singapore, with several days sailing ahead of us.

'Nothing happened all day but, the following morning the position of the remains were again found to be reversed. Neither my Staff Sergeant or myself had seen or heard anything; nobody had come on deck; we had remained all night watching the remains, talking and smoking; we were observed by the Skipper from the wheelhouse all the time and, there was no possibility of all three of us having even dozed, let alone fallen asleep.

'Perhaps there is a supernatural force at work.'

Strange ... But true. But that is not the end of the story. Let me first add that Captain Jones and his men were at sea for a total of one month - two weeks out and two weeks back to Singapore. That would mean, after other calls, about one week with the corpses which, were handed over to the War Graves Authorities in Singapore.

Major Jones returned to England in 1948 and, many times pondered over the strange eerie incident of Frankie and Johnny. In 1966 he sent to General T.C. Lethbridge at the institute of Psychic Research. 'I received a long reply dated 27 July 1966,' said Major Jones, 'in which he said that the whole thing was perfectly natural - normal - and probably a seaman with 'small powers' had wished the corpses elsewhere but only managed to change their positions.'

That I do not accept, nor did Major Jones. To do it once ... might be able to think it was the answer. But to do it six times ... you must look for a supernatural answer.

Lethbridge based his reply on Professor Rhine's research. He said that he had reasonably demonstrated that such things can be done by mental power alone. Thus the incident of Frankie and Johnny can be classified under the heading of poltergeist phenomena. And, said he would plump for one of the superstitious crew who, was unkowingly responsible for changing the positions of the corpses.

But that answer I do not accept and, it is the supernatural world that provides the answer to the Ghosts of the South China Seas.

STRANGE HAPPENINGS AT RAF SOERABAJA

On another occasion in 1946, Captain Jones was sent to investigate the crash of an RAF bomber at RAF Soerabaja.

The bomber, a Vultee Vengeance, had mysteriously crashed on the airfield and the crew suspected of being murdered. It is interesting to note that No 84 Squadron was using its Vengeance bombers to bomb the Japanese just south of Homalin, in Burma, when suddenly, they were taken off operations with the old Vultee Vegeance bomber and re-equipped with de Havilland Mosquitoes. But they had a sinister problem with the Mosquitoes and, for some unknown reason, they were withdrawn and, were never used against the Japanese.

Captain Jones and two Australians on one of the South Sea islands on route to RAF Soerabaja.

'A great pity,' said Corporal Smith of the RAF Ground Staff. 'The old Mossie would have blasted the yellow bastards off the face of the earth.'

At this period Captain Jones was stationed at Sonoabaya in Eastern Java while most of his unit remained at Singapore. For that reason he had to use Japanese prisoners-of-war as labour and, it was they who made the twelve coffins. Captain Jones explains:

'The boxes were about six feet by two feet by eighteen inches, simple and plain. We had completed our gruesome task, putting what remains could be found into the plain coffins and, I was just taking a rest.

'Suddenly one of the coffins started 'walking' away ... on to one side then its front, then the other side, then its back ... and so on. We all froze in utter amazement. Nobody was nearer than six to eight feet at the time, mostly sitting down resting. After the initial shock of seeing the coffin 'walking' away, the Japs fled and I had to bring them back by firing over their heads.

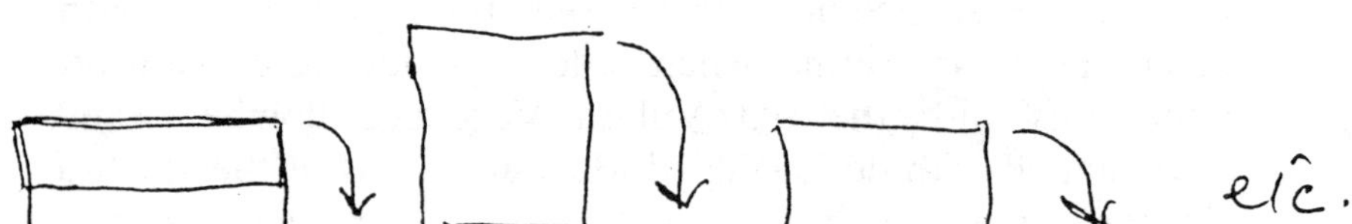

Drawing by Captain Jones to show movement of 'walking coffin'.

'The reason? Your guess is as good as mine. It could not have been the sun warping the wood for the coffin did not falter in its movement and only came to a halt after hitting a case some thirty feet away.'

So what made the coffin walk in the noonday sun at RAF Soerabaja..? Were those murdered by the despicable Japanese trying to haunt them? It is a fact that the Japanese are great believers in the vengeance of their ancestors. And, the Japanese have a lot to answer for. Let us look at the facts and hear what the Right Honourable Anthony Eden, Secretary of State for Foreign Affairs had to say in 1944.

Speaking in the House of Commons on 28th January, 1944, on the treatment of allied prisoners in the hands of the Japanese. Mr Anthony Eden said:

'I fear I have grave news to give the House. Members will be aware that a large number of postcards and letters have recently been received in this country from prisoners in the Far East; and that these almost uniformly suggest that the writers are being treated well and are in good health. There is no doubt from what we know about particular areas that some of these communications, at any rate, are in terms dictated by the Japanese authorities. I regret to have to tell the House that information which has been reaching his Majesty's Government no longer leaves room for any doubt that the true state of affairs is a very different one so far as the great majority of prisoners in Japanese hands is concerned.

'The House is already aware that a very high proportion, perhaps 80 to 90 per cent, of the prisoners and civilian internees in Japanese hands are located in the southern area, comprising the Philipine Islands, the Netherlands, East Indies, Borneo, Malaya, Burma, Siam, and Indo-China, and that the Japanese Government have hitherto withheld permission for any neutral inspection of any of the camps in question. We have not even been allowed to know the numbers of prisoners detained in the various areas, nor have the names of a large number of those who must have been taken prisoner by the Japanese yet been communicated to us.

'For some time past information has been reaching his Majesty's Government regarding the conditions under which prisoners are detained and worked in some of these areas, and as it was of so grave a character as to be likely to cause distress to relatives of prisoners and civilian internees in Japanese hands his Majesty's Government felt bound to satisfy themselves that it was authentic before making it public. We are now so satisfied, and it becomes my painful duty to tell the House that in Siam there are many thousands of prisoners from the British Commonwealth, including India, who are being compelled by the Japanese military to live in tropical jungle conditions without adequate shelter, clothing, food, or medical attention; and these men are forced to work on building a railway and making roads. Our information is that their health is rapidly deteriorating, that a high percentage are seriously ill, and that there have been some thousands of deaths. Here may I add that the number of such deaths reported by the Japanese to us is just over 100. The railway and roads concerned lead into Burma, and the conditions I have described apply throughout there whole length.

'One eye-witness reports of a camp in Siam that 'I saw many prisoners clearly; they were skin and bone, unshaven and with long matted hair; they were half-naked.' The same witness reported that they wore no hats or shoes; and this, may I remind the House, in a tropical climate, where the neighbouring country is virtually uninhabited, so that there are practically no local resources which could provide medical or other material relief.

'Of one other part of this huge southern area we have some information. From Java comes evidence which leaves no doubt that many of our prisoners are confined in camps with no adequate protection from malarial infection and lacking in proper provision for sanitation; except in so far as prisoners may sometimes obtain food from local sources, the food and clothing provided is insufficient to maintain them in health. Reports from the northern area have referred to the emaciated state of prisoners arriving from Java. I have so far no information to give the House regarding conditions in other parts of the Southern area.

'Before I leave the Southern area, there is one exception I can make to what I have said. There are civilians interned in our old military camp at Changi and in the neighbourhood of Bangkok and Saigon, and our information suggests that conditions of those particular camps are at least tolerable.

'The refusal of the Japenese Government to permit neutral inspections of camps in the southern area is difficult to understand, in view of the fact that they have allowed visits by neutral inspectors, though on a scale which we cannot regard as adequate, to camps in the northern area, which comprises Hong Kong, Formosa, Shanghai, Korea, and Japan itself. His Majesty's Government are reasonably satisfied that conditions generally in this area are tolerable, though as the Secretary of State for War has said on more than one occasion, the scale on which food is provided is not adequate over long periods to maintain the health of prisoners. I should add, however, that conditions in Hong Kong appear to be growing worse.

'If that were the whole of the story it would be bad indeed; but there is unhappily worse to come. We have a growing list of cases of brutal outrage on individuals or groups of individuals. I could not burden the House with the full tale of these. But in order to give an idea of their nature I must, I fear, quote a few typical examples. First, two cases affecting civilians.

'The first is that of an officer in the Shanghai Municipal Police Force. Along with some 200 other allied nationals he was interned by the Japanese in the dentention camp for so-called 'political suspects' at Haiphong Road in Shanghai. He incurred the displeasure of the Japanese gendarmerie and was taken away to their office in another part of the town. When he emerged from the building he was practically out of his mind; his arms and feet were infected where ropes had left deep scars; and he had lost 40 lb of weight. He died within a day or two of his release.

'The second case comes from the Philippine Islands. Here, on 11th February, 1942, three British subjects escaped from the Japanese civilian internment camp at Santo Tomas, Manila. They were recaptured and flogged by the camp guard. Two days later, on 14th February, they were sentenced to death by a military court, despite the fact that international law prescribes the imposition of only disciplinary punishment for attempts to escape. The firing party used automatic pistols, and the three men were not killed outright.

'I now turn to cases affecting soldiers. A number of Indian soldiers captured in Burma, having had their hands tied behind their backs, were made to sit in groups by the side of the road. They were then systematically bayoneted from behind in turn, each man receiving apparently three bayonet thrusts. By some miracle, one man who collapsed subsequently recovered and escaped to our lines. That's how we know.

'The other case concerns an officer of a well-known regiment of the line, who was captured in Burma. After being clubbed across the face with a sword he was tied to a stake and a rope was passed round his neck so that only by raising his body could he just get enough air to keep him alive. He was then subjected to further torture. Fortunately an allied attack developed, the Japanese fled, and the officer was rescued by a British tank.

'The third case concerns a transport called the Lisbon Maru which was being used to convey over 1,800 British prisoners of war from Hong Kong. Conditions on board were almost indescribable. The prisoners were seriously overcrowed. Many of them were undernourished and many had contracted diphtheria, dysentery, and other diseases. There was no medical provision; and the sanitary arrangements were virtually non-existent. Two of the prisoners in one hold died where they lay, and no attempt was made to remove their bodies.

'On the morning of 1st October, 1942, the vessel was torpedoed by a United Nations submarine. The Japanese officers, soldiers, and crew kept the prisoners under hatches and abandoned ship forthwith, although she did not sink until 24 hours later. There were unsufficient lifebelts and other safety appliances on board. Some of the prisoners managed to break out and swim to land. They were fired on when in the water. In all, at least 800 prisoners lost their lives.

'I have said sufficient to show the barbarous nature of our Japanese enemy. He has violated not only the principles of international law but all canons of decent and civilised conduct. His Majesty's Government have repeatedly made the strongest possible representations to the Japanese Government through the Swiss Government. Such replies as have been received have been evasive, cynical, or otherwise unsatisfactory. We had the right to expect that, once aware of the facts, the Japanese Government would remedy this state of affairs. The Japanese know well what are the obligations of a civilised Power to safeguard the life and health of prisoners who have fallen into their hands. This was shown by their treatment of prisoners in the Russo-Japanese war and the war of 1914-1918. Let the Japanese Government reflect that in time to come the record of their military authorities in this war will not be forgotten.

'It is with the deepest regret that I have been obliged to make such a statement to the House. But after consultation with their allies who are equally victims of this unspeakable savagery, his Majesty's Government have felt it to be their duty to make public the facts.'

Those are the facts... That is the reason why the coffin walked ... It was in shame for Jap atrocities of war are glossed over. In 1945, a defeated Japan that had inflicted horrendous atrocities on all prisoners of war and, their Asian neighbours expected the worse from the conquering heroes. By this period Eden was dancing to the American tune. What about war crimes? Instead the Americans made them what they are today. But what about them being tried for war crimes? The Germans were and, still are, as we have seen recently in Israel ... That is why the coffin 'walked' at RAF Soerabaja.

THE HAUNTED SQUADRON

In April 1931 No 40 Squadron was reformed as a bomber squadron at Upper Heyford ... the squadron badge being a broom and, it was not long before it became known as the haunted squadron with the broom taking on a more sinister meaning.

During the first world war No 40 Squadron had served on the Western Front as a fighter squadron. It disbanded in 1919.

On 26 September 1933, No 40 Bomber Squadron was returning to its home base at RAF Abingdon in Berkshire after exercises in Scotland. During these exercises the Squadron had used the old Royal Flying Club aerodrome at Montrose. No 40 Bomber Squadron was the first service squadron to use the airfield as a base since the eerie disaster that depleted No 2 Squadron in 1914.

As No 40 Bomber Squadron flew southwards that September morning in 1933 a strange supernatural event began to unfold ... almost a re-run of No 2 Squadrons disaster who, had returned at the same time ... Flight Sergeant Christian and his passenger in Fairey Gordon K1732 encountered thick mist over Northumberland and disappeared.

The earlier incident was in 1914. No 2 Squadron left Montrose and headed south for Netheravon on Salisbury Plain on 15 May 1914. They were to take part in exercises but, over Yorkshire they flew into thick ground mist. Lieutenant John Empson and A. G. Cudmore in a B. E. 2A, No 331, attempted to land at Hutton Bonville near Northallerton. The aircraft went through a hedge and overturned, killing Empson and Cudmore in the process.

After an almost identical disaster with No 40 Bomber Squadron many high ranking people linked the accident to the supernatural influence associated with the old aerodrome at Montrose. Still fresh in the minds of many Service Personnel being the ghost of Montrose Aerodrome.

But the 40 Squadron incident was much more mysterious. A day after aircraft Fairey Gordon K1732 disappeared, an aircraft wheel was washed up on the East Coast and Christian's body floated in three days later. The body of his passenger was never found.

And stranger still ... aircraft K1732 was never on charge to 40 Squadron. It was struck off charge on ... 26 September 1933. The very day this aircraft is said to have crashed. How very, very strange.

THE NEWALL HOUSE PHANTOM

And there are ghostly goings-on at the old Officers' Mess at present day RAF Waddington, as I was to find out during my visit.

In August 1991 I paid a visit to RAF Waddington to see Flying Officer Nicky Tilmouth WRAF. 'It all started when I wrote to the publishers of the books and was subsequently treated to a personal visit from Mr Barrymore Halpenny and his son Baron,' she said.

Lancaster bomber on dispersal.

When I arrived in the office of Flying Officer Nicky Tilmouth, the station's community relations officer, I was introduced to Nicky Pearson, the wife of an RAF police dog handler - and also a Ghost Stations fan - and she had her own ghostly story to tell me.

'Newall House at RAF Waddington is haunted,' said Nicky Pearson. 'Many ghostly sighting have been reported.'

Flying Officer Nicky Tilmouth nodded her head to confirm it was true.

Nicky Pearson continued. 'My colleague, Sue Cox was alone in Newall House one night when she saw a man between the two flights of stairs.

'Thinking it was an intruder she tried to catch up with him ... but he had vanished into thin air. Knowing that she had clearly seen someone, she informed the RAF Station police but, after a very thorough search they found no-one.'

Newall House at RAF Waddington is the standard type building on airfields built during the expansion period between the wars. The one at RAF Waddington was built in 1929 and in use as an Officers' Mess until the mid-fifties.

Now all is empty ... The Operations Room stands silent. Now only the ghosts from the past remain.

Over coffee and biscuits, Nicky continued. 'I have often felt a 'presence' in many of the buildings, particularly Newall House. And there is the haunted cash box that mysteriously moves from one filing cabinet to another. It is all very weird,' she said.

She went on to say: 'And people in Newall House, including myself, have suddenly felt it go very cold. Also, lights switch on and off - yet no one is anywhere near any of the switches.'

And Nicky Tilmouth added: 'We do know that there are many other ghosts at RAF Waddington. And we are both very intrigued about the phantom in Newall House.'

Yes, there are many unexplained happenings at RAF Waddington as Readers of my Ghost Stations books are well aware. And, the phantom of Newall House just another in search of his comrades of the second world war.

THE GREMLINS

Number 431 (Iroquois) Squadron, Royal Canadian Air Force, formed at Burn in Yorkshire in November 1942, as a bomber squadron of No4 Group.

In July 1943, it was transferred to No 6 Group Royal Canadian Air Force and, moved to Tholthorpe.

The squadron was equipped with four-engined Halifaxes and the squadron's badge was an Iroquois Indian's head.

Tholthorpe airfield had been allocated to the Canadians and when it reopened in June 1943 it was part of No 6 Group. The first occupants being No 434 (Bluenose) Squadron RCAF which formed at Tholthorpe. Followed quickly by 431 Squadron who began to workup to operations with their Halifax bombers, one of them being Halifax LK 640 Q for Queenie which, soon sported a picture of Queenie on its nose.

Halifax LK640 on dispersal ... the ground crew hard at work to remove the Gremlins.

Q-Queenie was a mighty beast with a proud crew ... but it was very temperamental. 'It was the Gremlins,' said the groundcrew. The engines would be fine, then for no apparent reason they would not be running right. Many times the groundcrew worked on the engines only to find nothing wrong.

Each time operations were on, the Gremlins would start to work on Q-Queenie. And, the groundcrew become frustrated, for Q-Queenie was a new aircraft and, they could never find anything wrong.

Was it the task that it was having to perform that caused the Gremlins to take over?

Then, one of the groundcrew said it had to be the dispersal that was haunted ... 'It always felt extra cold on that dispersal,' he said.

All minor repairs on all bombers were carried out on the dispersals. Only major repairs were carried out in the hangar. All work on Q-Queenie was therefore carried out on the dispersal.

But it was not just the dispersal, the whole airfield was unlucky for both 431 and 434 Squadrons.

Then, came news that the squadron might be moving to Croft. The groundcrew of Q-Queenie were pleased with the news and they patted the old bomber.

Again the groundcrew worked to rid the bomber of its Gremlins ... then came the news of maximum effort and Q-Queenie was declared operational. Their target, the I.G. Farben factories at Ludwigshaven, which, had been bombed during August and September but, had escaped lightly during three major raids.

Each attack on Ludwigshaven had been a costly failure. Now it was the turn of 431 Squadron and Q-Queenie was put through her night-flying test. Then the routine engine and airframe checks, radio and radar equipment, guns, turrets, hydraulic system, instruments, oxygen apparatus, and bomb-release and electrical systems.

'I just had a feeling I would not see Q-Queenie again,' said a fitter. That feeling was true ... Q-Queenie failed to return from Ludwigshaven. On 19 November 1943, Q-Queenie clawed its way into the night sky and was never seen again.

THE PHANTOM PILOT

After a bomber role during the war years, RAF Middleton St. George - known as Goosepool - became a fighter airfield in June 1956 and its operational life started in this new role when the Hawker Hunter F6s of 92 Squadron and, the Gloster Meteor NF 14s of 264 Squadron arrived in March 1957. Both units stayed until the following September.

Shortly after the departure of these two jet-fighter squadrons a Phantom Pilot was seen in and around the Mess area. Almost everyone who has seen the Phantom Pilot say the phantom figure looks real but ashen, as if dazed and, is wearing flying kit.

It is possible, from the many eyewitness reports, for the details never seem to vary; that the Phantom Pilot is that of a National Service pilot who crashed his Meteor Jet whilst training.

Apparently he had landed for a 'touch and go' on the old 10 - 28 runway which, now houses the air terminal, when an engine cut out. There is some speculation as to whether the pilot was aware of this occurrence as he attempted to take off with full power on the remaining engine.

This, I am reliably informed by a pilot who was there at the time, that this was a definite 'no no' with the twin-engined Meteor Jet ... and it proved to be so for the aircraft became uncontrollable, slewed off the runway and continued the relatively short distance to the Mess, striking a parked car on the way. The Jet Fighter crashed into the Mess wall, dislodging some masonry which fell through the canopy and killed the pilot. The crash led to a string of very strange events ... eerie events which could be why the Phantom Pilot haunts the airfield.

A Meteor Jet of the type which crashed into the Mess wall.

It was very strange that the motor car which was damaged in the crash ... belonged to the pilot. And, the section of the Mess into which the Meteor Jet crashed ... was the pilot's own room. And if that was not enough ... the term used by Meteor Pilots when their Meteor suddenly dropped one wing - for there was a tendancy for the Meteor to drop one wing quite suddenly - was ... phantom roll.

THE GRINDON GHOSTS

Grindon is a remote moorland village in the Peak National Park and due to its height above sea level (800 ft) is frequently covered by low clouds and mist. In severe winters it is often cut off from the outside world by snow. The severe winter of 1947 was one such winter.

On Thursday 13th February, 1947, Halifax RT922, a four-engined bomber of No 47 Glider Towing Squadron, code letters MOHD, based at Fairford in Gloucestershire, crashed on Grindon Moor in Staffordshire, some eight miles east of Leek, whilst dropping hay in snow. All onboard, including a number of pressmen were killed.

A memorial window was erected in Grindon Church and pieces of the wreckage dug up by aviation archeologists can be found on a display board in The Cavalier Inn located in the centre of the village.

The haunted Cavalier Inn at Grindon and home for the Grindon Ghosts

The inn is an old building erected in the late 17th century and has been a public house for over 100 years. Formerly called the Shoulder of Mutton probably when sheep drovers stopped while en route to market, the inn was renamed the Cavalier by a previous owner some 30 years ago.

In February 1988, Bob Blunden purchased the Inn and, it was not long before he began to hear about the alleged hauntings. The locals told of a grey haired man dressed in grey who would walk down the stairs from the private accommodation, walked along the front of the bar and disappeared into the dining-room. One barmaid had fled the Inn on seeing this apparition.

'Initially we treated the stories with some cynicism until we began to note various occurrences,' said Bob Blunden. 'Glasses would move off the shelves and crash to the floor. One Thursday evening a sherry barrel on a shelf behind the bar was lifted above the surrounding bottles and similarly crashed to the floor. This was witnessed by several customers. We also discovered that one of the reasons the previous owners sold was because the wife was scared of the 'ghost.'

'On other days there would be a smell at the end of the bar akin to rotting compost which I could smell but my wife could not. Similarly when resting upstairs in the private lounge my wife frequently complained about a horrible smell and from her description it was the same as the smell that I experienced in the bar.

'On many occasions as we closed up for the night we heard a small child's voice come from the dining room saying 'nite, nite' and we both felt a presence on the stairs of a small animal. Frequently the heavy inner door to the main bar would open and close yet nobody entered the pub.

'One Bank Holiday we were talking to some customers about our experiences and they decided not to tell us that their daughter who, was allegedly psychic, was visiting them the following day.

'The following day I noted the customers talking to their daughter, all sitting on an old leather settle in the dining room, when suddenly a suit of armour at the end of the dining room fell over with a loud crash. The daughter said that she saw a little boy push it ... yet there was nobody else in the dining room.

'Glasses continued to crash to the floor and a pint mug would suddenly start to swing like mad on the hooks above the bar. In addition the beer would mysteriously switch off in the cellar.

'Then one night after we had retired we awoke to my son screaming. On climbing up to his bedroom in the attic he was screaming 'keep her away from me.' We comforted him and told him he was dreaming, but further investigation revealed that Roy Shenton, a previous barman at the pub had slept in the same room and had experienced visitations from a woman with long grey hair dressed in a long black dress. He said that she used to sit on the end of his bed and he used to pull the covers over his head hoping that she would go away. Eventually he ended up having medical treatment as his nerves got so bad.

'The smells and disturbances continued until we left the pub in June 1990. As far as I am aware they continue to this day.'

BLOTTING OUT THE PAST

'Having just obtained the three Ghost Stations books, it is Hornchurch and North Weald entries which prompted me to contact you,' said Desmond Keen.

And Desmond's information may help many of my Readers understand why the old airfields have a 'tear on the wind', as their heroic past was sadly blotted out.

Desmond Keen continues: 'As a mere National Service shorthand-typist, my first posting was to the Aviation Candidates Selection Boards at RAF Hornchurch in October 1946.

'I had previously been stationed at Euston House in London, it was here only a lodger unit housed in the central hangar, which always seemed like a great empty cathedral to me. All one could see from the office windows on those late winter afternoons was the grim approach of the evening mists over the deserted airfield ... no one ever spoke to us of the wartime glories of the place.

'The iron hand of authority seemed anxious to blot out the station's battle experiences and return everything to 'pre-war RAF standards.

'I remember seeing the last of the aircrew wall-painting being obliterated from the old barrack blocks on the square soon after I got there.

'The ACSB staff lamented the loss of their convenient spot in London and morale was poor - especially as we suffered the 1947 winter there. The unit was moved to North

Weald in April 1947 - reasons unknown - and then, to our dismay, we had to return to Hornchurch in October 1948.

'By then the name had been changed to the Combined Selection Centre - CSC and, it is at this point I was puzzled by the entry in Book One (page 154) which refers to a 'large rambling building on the edge of the airfield. It had formerly been used as the Officers' Mess.'

'We understood that it was the sergeants who had all been evicted from their fine modern premises - much bad feeling - in order to provide us with offices and interview rooms, as the work had grown and the hangar offices were inadequate.

'I remained there until March 1949 and once again for me and my friends, it was an unhappy place.'

And because they squashed the memories of those gallant airmen ... they return ... like the Ghost of Montrose ... to haunt the old airfields.

MORE HAUNTINGS AT RAF LEEMING

In Book Four of Ghost Stations there is a story 'The Most Haunted Airfield - RAF Leeming and, the old airfield continues to live up to that title.

In Book One Ghost Stations we have the story 'The Ghosts of RAF Leeming' and, in that story, I do explain the history of the wartime airfield so that Readers can understand the role it played and, understand the sadness and sorrow. It is therefore easy to understand the hauntings by the phantom aircrews.

A few years ago an army military bandsman was staying with the band at RAF Leeming. They had practiced hard during the day and were taking a well earned drink in the bar that evening when suddenly, a military policeman rushed into the bar.

'He looked terrified,' said the army bandsman. 'He then blurted out that whilst doing his security round the lights had come on in the hangar that he knew was locked ... and no one was inside!'

It transpired that the lights had come on, in what was known on the Station, as the haunted hangar. And, the Station policeman had quickly gone to get help ... partly if it was an intruder help would be on hand ... but also prove that there was a supernatural force, should no intruder be found.

When the back-up force arrived at the hangar in question ... sure enough, the hangar lights were on. And, after checking that the hangar was still securely locked with no visible points of entry, the Sergeant decided that it was someone playing the fool ... knowing it was the alleged haunted hangar.

However, to be on the safe side, he put in two trained police dogs in order to calm everyone's nerves.

'We will leave the dogs in for the rest of the night,' he said. 'And take them out at shift change in the morning.'

The following morning, needless to say, the dogs had to be destroyed.

The hangar in question was well known for its strange and eerie atmosphere. In certain sections it would suddenly go very cold. And tools would go missing.

Many of those who have worked in the haunted hangar believe it is the ghosts of the two crew members of a Gloster Javelin Jet fighter that had crashed on landing, killing both crew. The wreckage of the jet had been stored in that hangar.

In June 1957 No 228 Operation Conversion Unit arrived at RAF Leeming and, it was tasked with the training of crews for the ever-increasing number of Javelin squadrons and the first course began in October 1957.

Then, much to the bewilderment of the staff, it was decided to disband 228 OCU in the late summer of 1961. The Javelin OCU had done an excellent job and the government thought there were enough trained Javelin crews but, it was another high-level blunder. The Javelin was to remain in service for seven more years, necessitating the reformation of other training units from 1963 onwards.

That could explain the haunting ... But there are so many unexplained happenings it is much more than just that one incident.

A telephone in the hangar keeps ringing and, when answered a chilling voice calls the name of an aircrew member ... They are the phantoms of RAF Leeming.

THE RED FOUR MYSTERY

When, on 27 May 1942, Field Marshal Erwin Rommel's Panzer Afrika Korps began to move forward it forestalled a British offensive already ordered to begin early in June, for which, General Claude Auchinleck had tried to husband forces. Immediately after the failure of the Axis attempt to break through to the Delta in September 1942, the British Eighth Army began to prepare for a full-scale offensive, timed to take place about the middle of October. For many days a fierce battle raged at El Alamein.

The part played by the Royal Air Force in the desert campaigns, was truly tremendous. The Desert Air Force and the Eighth Army were one big fighting family, working with a single purpose, to destroy Rommel's Afrika Korps.

The Royal Air Force in the Western Desert had a very difficult task ... what may be called the cinema impression of a desert is nothing like the Western Desert. The sandstorms so often mentioned are more frequently choking clouds of dust rather than sand. Vast stretches are hard, firm going ... except after rain ... and resemble flat rock more than anything else. Among the more disagreeable features are the flies. They are a filthy, pertinacious, excruciating pestilence. When General Von Ravenstein, commander of the 21st German Armoured Division was captured he said 'The desert is the tactician's paradise but, the quartermaster's hell!'

Those of the Desert Air Force ... nicknamed the Flying Desert Rats ... had more than just the heat of the battle to contend with. Their desert base was just a sand landing strip ...

no concrete, tarmac or grass runways ... There were over two hundred Landing Grounds, LGs for short, in North Africa and very few of them had names, usually it was just a number. Some existed for years, others only a few days. Their base consisted of just a sand strip surrounded by featureless desert. No buildings ... just a few tents. All RAF fighter squadrons had only one 'Pilots Mess Tent' when on operations. This was used by all pilots and any other officers and usually consisted of some thirty personnel.

Edward Stott, 33 Squadron, who witnessed the Red Four mystery.

On Monday 27 July 1942, twelve hurricane fighters of 'A' Flight, No 33 Squadron took off from Landing Ground 92 for a dawn patrol over El Alamein. Their flight brief - A fighter 'sweep' over El Alamein at 'Angels One Five'. And for the uninitiated, that is 15,000 feet. One of those Flying Desert Rats on that dawn patrol was Sergeant Edward Stott. 'We met no enemy fighters on this patrol but half way back to base it was noted that Red Four was lagging behind the formation,' he said.

Red Four was the code-name for Sergeant Pilot Leicester, a new pilot with the squadron who, was on his first desert dawn patrol.

Edward Stott continues: 'My Flight Commander, Flight Lieutenant Lance Wade, the famous American Ace fighter pilot, quickly issued a command: 'Red Leader to Red Four, Catch up. Catch up ... you are too far behind'.

'This command was shortly repeated: 'Red Leader to Red Four ... Catch up formation and hold your position.' But Red Four continued to drop further and further behind. Suddenly two Messerschmitt 109s were seen above and behind us. They dived on Red Four and he was shot down in flames.

'We returned to base and landed, then went to the Mess Tent for our delayed breakfast. Here we met 'B' Flight who had by now finished their breakfast. We discussed our flight and the sad loss of young Sergeant Pilot Leicester. They looked very surprized and said we must be mistaken.

'And why should we be mistaken? we asked. And they replied almost in unison, 'Because Sergeant Leicester had breakfast with us here half-an-hour ago!'

The pilots of 'B' Flight were adamant that they had all seen Sergeant Leicester and their stance only deepened the mystery of Red Four.

Edward Stott continues with the now deeply baffling Red Four mystery: 'The 'B' Flight pilots claim that Sergeant Leicester had indeed breakfasted with them was confirmed by several officers who were present in the Mess Tent. They were completely mystified by my denial which, was backed up by my colleagues when we insisted that it was impossible for the young pilot to have been in the Mess Tent that morning because they in turn had seen Sergeant Leicester's Hurricane fighter disappear in flames.

' 'B' Flight finally accepted the loss of the new pilot. But all the officers who were witnesses to the incident were deeply puzzled by it.'

Sergeant Pilot Edward Stott went on to fly Spitfires with No 145 Squadron, Desert Air Force, the Squadron Leader commanding the squadron being none other than my good friend Neville Duke - featured in my first Ghost Stations (page 98) and in my Ghost Stations II (page 154 - 155 with his photograph on 155 also). Edward Stott spent four-and-a-half years in the Middle East. Today, he is a retired aircraft design engineer.

His early Flight Commander became Wing Commander Lance Wade, winning the Distinguished Flying Cross with two Bars and the Distinguished Service Order. He was killed in a flying accident in Italy on Thursday 13 January 1944.

THE COLLEGE ROAD GHOST

'I have just finished reading your book Ghost Stations III,' said Derek Smith. 'I found the little bit about Hornchurch interesting as I now live very near the old Hornchurch fighter station. Also the story about Hendon for in 1957 I spent thirteen weeks at Hendon Police College which, I believe at that time used a lot of the old buildings belonging to Hendon Airfield, as a mess hall and dormitories etcetera.

'I regret to say nothing I saw in that thirteen weeks was in the least bit ghostly. However, I do have a story which happened to me when I was a child and, I thought that it was about time I told someone about it, before it gets put down to the ramblings of an old man.'

Derek Smith's story is such an interesting one that I had to include it. It is not one with airfields, nevertheless, it does have some bearing, from the fact of being able to understand the reason behind the ghostly visit, in this case, the jawbone.

I would like to make clear that the house in which Derek Smith then lived, No. 19 College Road, was originally gas lit and, the fittings for the electric light were all converted gas mantles fitted to the wall. His bedroom was at the back of the house and the ceiling sloped with the roof line. Thus, the only place for his bed was in front of the door, the window was at the foot of the bed slightly to the left.

Derek Smith continues:

'I was born on the 11th of September 1938, in a small two up and two down wooden weatherboarded cottage, in College Road, Epsom, Surrey. I lived in that cottage with my parents and younger sister until I was fouteen years, when we all moved to a council house on the other side of the town.

'When I was ten or eleven years old, I was helping my father to dig a plot in the garden, ready for planting, when I turned up a lower human jaw bone, complete with teeth. I cleaned it under the tap to free it of the chalky soil, which was adhering to it and, took it into the house.

'I thought no more of it, and my father said we should take it to the police the following day. I went to bed that night at my normal time and fell asleep.

'I woke up suddenly during the night, the moon was up and was shining through the small window, at the foot of my bed. In the light, standing next to my bed, (which was the old fashioned kind with head and footboards and a metal frame,) was the figure of a man. He was about five feet ten and dressed in Cavalier dress, a large hat with feather, knee breeches, a sort of short jacket or coat over his right shoulder and, a shirt with puffed sleeves. But the funny thing was that he was grey, and semitransparent, yet he looked solid.

'I took all this in, in the few seconds that I looked at him. The only way out of my small bedroom, without touching the figure was over the headboard which, is the way I went, without taking my eyes from the figure. I hit the light switch and the figure vanished.

'I woke my parents who, told me it was just the moonlight, shining through the net curtain, over my window. I did not believe them and, I do not think that they believed it either.

'The following day, the jawbone was reburied deeply in the garden and, although I was frightened, I had to sleep in that bedroom for the next few years until we moved house. I never saw anything else in my bedroom and, although the moonlight continued to shine through my window at night, it never again took on human shape.

'I firmly believe that I saw the ghost owner of that lower jaw and, that he wanted it put back into the earth where, I presume, that the rest of his body was buried.

'My parents told nobody of my experience, so if the cottages are still there and, the area has not been redeveloped, I would think that he still lies under the ground, in the cottage garden.'

LILI MARLEEN, THE HAUNTING WARTIME SONG

Lili Marleen ... the haunting song of the second world war. It was Lale Anderson's haunting voice that introduced Lili Marleen to the German Africa Korps and, the British troops heard it sung by captured German soldiers. And such was the impact of this haunting song on the troops that the British government commissioned Tommie Conner to produce English lyrics for the music.

The haunting Lili Marleen swept all Theatres of War ... It was blowing on the wind. Those fighting in Italy were called D-Day Dodgers by Lady Astor, Britain's first woman member of parliament who, had visited Italy in October 1944 to examine the soldier's living conditions. She then made a statement saying the troops spent too much time on drunken orgies and, that the VD rate was so high that all troops who were in Italy should be made to wear yellow armbands (is that what they mean?) so that 'British Womanhood' could indentify them and, thereby avoid them. Great damage was done by these allegations which caused great resentment among the troops. This led to a poem being written by someone at Eighth Army HQ. The poem was put to the tune of Lili Marleen and a printed copy was sent to all soldiers in the Eighth Army.

Many, if not all the readers will remember the wartime Lili Marleen song and, some of you the song of the D-Day Dodgers; but for the benefit of those who are not familiar with it, here it is:

The Song of the D-Day Dodgers - sung to the tune of 'Lili Marleen'.

We're the D-Day Dodgers' out in Italy,
Always on the vino and always on the spree,
Eighth Army scroungers and their tanks,
We live in Rome amongst the Yanks,
We're the D-Day dodgers in sunny Italy.

We landed at Śalerno a holiday with pay,
The Gerries brought the bands out to cheer us on our way,
Showed us the sights and gave us tea,
We all sang songs and the beer was free,
To welcome D-Day dodgers to sunny Italy.

Naples and Casino we've taken in our stride,
We didn't come to fight here we just came for the ride,
Anzio and Sangro were just names,
We only came to look for dames,
The randy D-Day dodgers in sunny Italy.

On the way to Florence we had a lovely time,
We ran a bus to Rimini right through the Gothic Line,
Soon to Bologna we will go,
And after that we'll cross the Po,
We'll still be D-Day dodging in sunny Italy.

Once we heard a rumour that we were going home,
Back to dear old Blighty and never more to roam,
Then someone said in France you'll fight,
We said no fear we'll just sit tight,
The windy D-Day dodgers in sunny Italy.

Dear Lady Astor you think you know a lot,
Standing on your platform and talking tommy rot,
You England's sweetheart and its pride,
We think your mouth's too bleeding wide,
That's from your D-Day dodgers in sunny Italy.

Look around the mountains in the mud and rain,
See the scattered crosses there's some which have no name,
Heartbreak and sorrow are all gone,
The boys beneath them slumber on,
They are the D-Day dodgers who'll stay in Italy.

And even at the bomber stations the haunting Lili Marleen crept in. In the public houses of Mablethorpe in Lincolnshire and elsewhere, the Boys from the bomber stations would sing the following to the tune of Lili Marleen.

Down in windy Lincolnshire down beside the sea,
There is a bomber squadron of which I'm proud to be,
Press on regardless is our cry,
To do or die, not to reason why,
The Boys of 619 the famous 619.

The enemy's coast ahead Boys,
Look at all the flak,
Mother dear I hope you're near,
Or else we'll n'ere get back.

The flare path's behind us, far behind,
It's cold up here,
But we don't mind,
We're pressing on regardless,
The Boys of 619 the famous 619.

But why had Lili Marleen such a haunting effect on just about all Allied and Axis troops ...? To find out the possible reason we must go back to the beginning.

Lili Marleen started life as a sad little poem in the first world war.

It was written by Hans Leip, a German soldier who had fought in the trenches and, who knew firsthand the horrors of war.

In 1917 Hans Leip fell in love with two young Fraulein's ... one was called Betty but Hans called her his 'Lili' ... the other young Fraulein was called Marleen.

Already the contents take on a haunting flavour as Hans, who was torn between the two young Fraulein's, brought them together in his poem - 'Lied Eines jungen Wachtpostens' - the theme being about a young soldier on sentry duty ... in the mind of Hans Leip it was a ghost soldier. The next spooky piece of the puzzle now in place.

For some unknown reason Norbert Schultze put the poem to music and, the eerie, haunting melody of Lili Marleen became an instant favourite after Lale Anderson sang Lili Marleen on Radio Cologne in 1939. It then surfaced again after a demand for records for Rommel's Afrika Korps in North Africa and it was played on Radio Belgrade on 18 August 1941. It became a cult amongst the hard fighting soldiers of the German Army ... but not with the German Officers who, all wished to dissociate and distance themselves for the haunting Lili Marleen.

How very, very strange ... and to add to the haunting mystery, Norbert Schultze - the German head of the Leon Jessel Foundation which, is named after a Jewish composer - alleged killed by the Nazis - also wants to dissociate himself from the haunting Lili Marleen ... He says he is ashamed of his wartime music ... Why?

When I contacted Norbert Schultze in 1990, he refused to reply to me, instead, I got a curt letter from Apollo-Verlag saying I could not use any Apollo-Verlag edition of Lili Marleen and, of Schultze, they said, 'Mr Schultze wishes not to be mentioned.'

Very nice. And why not ..? Is it because he did not want to admit that he still receives about **TWELVE THOUSAND POUNDS STERLING** a year in royalties from Lili Marleen ... no wonder it is a haunting Lili Marleen!

Should any war pensioner who, is haunted by the wartime Lili Marleen song but, does not get the pot of gold at the end of the rainbow, drop Mr Schultze a line at Humboldtstr, 9, D-1000 Berlin 33, Germany. Or give him a call ... 010. 49. 30. 8913793 ... and remind him of Lili Marleen ... that eerie, haunting wartime song.

GLENN MILLER

After my Ghost Stations IV hit the bookshops, a flood of letters to support and, congratulate me on exposing the TRUTH about Major Glenn Miller ... but one arrived with fangs exposed, from a professional author. And from his letter I will prove which end he is talking from.

I have reproduced Wilbur Wright's letter in full and answered same in numerical order of the letter.

I served, as stated in many of my books, in the Royal Air Force Provost Special Security and, one of the few stationed on the purpose built Atomic Bomb-Storage Site. The only one of its kind in the world... a plan of the Station shown for the **FIRST** time in my ACTION STATIONS 8 Military Airfields of Greater London, page 266. My credentials.

Miller with American singer Irene Manning. US Army photograph taken during their broadcast in London in November 1944.

Dear Mr. Halpenny -

GHOST STATIONS 4 - GLENN MILLER

I trust you will have no objection to my making some comments on your above story - I have been researching the Miller mystery for 6 years and I am a professional author with 14 published books including one best-seller. I append hereunder the true documented story of Miller's disappearance with some photocopies which may be of interest. With regard to your own story -

1) You say Miller was a spy. For or against the Americans? Or for or against the British? You omit to say. The item about his broadcasts containing coded messages was first publicised in the Frank Wappat tape of 1991 - the BBC admitted that their record archives were vandalised and robbed post-war when they were moved to Reading, and items stolen included all Miller's wartime discs. His broadcasts were analysed by the scientific establishment at Bletchley Park and were found to contain nothing suspicious.

2) You say Don Haynes' diary was totally fictitious - yet you quote from it at length inferring that was the real course of events up to Friday December 15 1944. We obtained copies of Miller's Burial File and 201 Personal File and Haynes' name is not mentioned in any official document, signal or record. As you say, it was fictitious -

3) I have John Morgan's full personal history and am in contact with his family. He had flown a total of 683 hours at his death, with no operational missions at all. He was based on a Ferry Squadron at R.A.F. Heston, Middlesex for a year after completing flying training at two R.A.F. bases, underwent a Beam Approach Training Course and transferred to the USAAF in early 1944. In September that year he was transferred from 44 Strategic Air Depot Wattisham to 35 Air Depot Repair Squadron, Abbotts Ripton. In November 1944 he flew 7 missions totalling 21 hours and in December 1944 flew only twice - on December

2nd returning from Paris with Baessell, and on Friday 15 December, his last flight.

4) Morgan was cleared direct to Base B-42 Beauvais France, and Bordeaux (I have his Service Record Card and copy of his orders) and he left Abbotts Ripton at 13.25 cleared direct to Beauvais, flying east of London to Dymchurch, Kent. He was spotted by a Royal Observer Corps lady who phoned in during a radio programme to confirm. The sighting was passed on to SHAEF, Versailles.

5) About 6 miles west of Le Touquet about 14-45 hours, the Norseman suffered a failure of the propeller hydraulic system causing a runway propeller which sheared off. He and Baessell, the only occupants, died from drowning. The aircraft was found by Clive Ward, oceanic survey expert, who found the propeller was missing. We traced 8 other C-64 aircraft missing in the ETO in 1944, and by a process of elimination that off Le Touquet can only be 44-70285, Morgan's aircraft.

6) For your information, the Station Form 540 Daily History for R.A.F. Twinwood Farm on 15 December 1944 reads Airfield closed. No flying today. We located three serving R.A.F. people based there that day, including Mr. Glover the Air Traffic Controller. All three state no Norseman landed there that day.

7) Lt.Col. Norman F. Baessell (note spelling) was not a pilot, or Goodrich's personal pilot. He was a staff officer, a Special Assistant to Goodrich responsible for locating, equipping and opening Advance Repair Bases (8th Air Force Service Command carried out the repair and servicing of all 8th AF aircraft). He met Miller fortuitously - the AAF Band moved to Bedford to escape the V1s and 8th AFSC HQ was at Milton Ernest Hall 3 miles out of town. His orders for 15 December were to fly to Beauvais, drop some spares, stay the night and fly to Bordeaux next day. Base Y-37 Bordeaux-Merignac had opened up on December 6 as an 8th AF medium bomber base and Baessell was going to inspect and determine their needs.

8) Your evidence about the WAAF Controller is totally incorrect. She was LACW Dixie Clerke, who settled in British Columbia after the war and died in 1988. Her date of birth was December 15 - the same day Miller allegedly vanished. We proved conclusively that she confused her dates - she witnessed the November 8 flight on which Morgan picked up Miller, Baessell and Haynes: Miller bound for Villacoublay and SHAEF, was dropped at Bovingdon and Morgan flew on to Orly with the others. I have an interview tape she made with a Mr. Ken Perfect in 1983.

9) Your account of the time spent at Twinwood waiting for Morgan is a straight extract from the Haynes diaries, one of which said Morgan came from Station 525 Heston and the other said Station 595 Honington. Morgan's flight records show he flew down from Honington on November 8, not December 15 - and Haynes used details from that account to fabricate his December 15 story. Morgan could not have been 'talked down' on the later date - the airfield was closed.

10) I spent much time at Oakley, Twinwood and Milton Ernest Hall on research. I met 11 people who worked at the R.A.E. and none were aware of any 'secret tunnels'.

11) You give no explanation of why Baessell and Morgan were involved. There is no evidence of any kind to support the Podington story. As a matter of fact, I have on record some 38 different accounts of Miller's fate, and all suffer from the same lack of solid documentary evidence.

12) In what international scandal was Miller involved? If he was such a morale asset as Doolittle described, why was it necessary to 'get rid of him'?

13) Your comment about the Burial Files is misleading. Burial Files are opened for all 'missing' US Army/Air Force personnel, even if their bodies are never recovered. I obtained Burial Files for Miller, Morgan and Baessell after appealing to President Reagan. There is no evidence in Miller's Buriel File or his 201 Personal File to support your story. Wing Commander Stidolph, like 20 or more people I

have met, was another glory-hunter prepared to invent the most outlandish stories - but significantly, several of the other people I have met admitted they were being paid to disseminate false information - in cash dollars in letters posted from Alexandria Virginia and Pasadena, California.

14) In March 1992 I located LACW Joan Heath, personal driver to Air Marshal Tedder at SHAEF Versailles in December 1944. Miller flew to Paris by shuttle from Bovingdon on Thursday December 14 accompained by Teddy Gower, resident BBC engineer, and a small group of musicians including Nat Peck, Mel Powell, Peanuts Hucko and Ray McKinley. On Saturday December 16 they played at a big party at SHAEF to celebrate Ike's promotion to General of the Army - Joan Heath was there and talked to Miller. He said he was going Stateside for a few days over Christmas and she agreed to take him to Buc Airfield, a mile from Versailles, used by 115th Liaison Squadron flying Cessna UC 78 Bobcats. On Sunday morning she drove Miller to the airfield and saw him board the plane : it was to take him to Bordeaux, where he would board a transAtlantic flight using the southerly route via the Azores. Bordeaux had been operational since December 6th. The Bobcat was lost en route and since Miller was AWOL (desertion in wartime) the loss was hushed up. The wreck and bodies were sighted in June 1946 from the air but not found despite a wide search. SHAEF had no idea of Miller's fate and because the Christmas Day broadcast to America was imminent, prepared the Norseman story with the help of Haynes.

15) Miller's body was eventually found and returned quietly to his family in California. Since Eisenhower (later President) was involved in the whole business, a cover-up was essential and is ongoing today. I know where he is buried, including Grave and Buriel Lot number and the address of the cemetery. His family want the secret kept because they believe Miller would be accused of desertion - he did not have permission to make the flight.

In conclusion, may I say on a personal note that I deplore your virulent anti-British comments in Ghost Stations 4 - again, totally unsupported by factual evidence. And for your information Napoleon died of cynanide poisoning by fumes emanated by the green dye in his wallpaper - St. Helena was warm and humid and his final illness bore all the hallmarks of cyanosis. One of his servants sent home a sample of the wallpaper in her scrap-book which was analysed and shown to contain a high level of cyanide.

The man who died in Spandau, of course, was not Hess - his body showed no trace of the gunshot wound he received in World War 1. The dead man was a double introduced by mutual 4-Power agreement to maintain the *status quo* as long as possible.

Yours sincerely

WILBUR WRIGHT

Major Miller looks wistfully at Corporal Ruby Newell.

So now let me answer Wright's letter. The photocopies referred to I will answer at 4.

1. Miller a spy? Against the Allies. Wright then says the item about Miller's broadcasts containing coded messages was first publicised in 1991.

I had that first. I said it in 1958. And first part of Miller story published in my Ghost Stations III first published April 1990. The concluding part of Miller in my Ghost Stations IV, first published in March 1991.

How very convenient to have all of Miller's wartime discs stolen!

And why should the scientific establishment at Bletchly Park want to analyse Miller's broadcasts?

2. As stated in my Ghost Stations IV, Don Haynes was the man who sowed the seeds of deception.

Wright says Haynes not mentioned in any official document. That does not mean a damn thing. It is a fact that Haynes was driving the Staff car. That is the important point.

3. So what!

Baesell lived to fly another day.

4. No Flight Plan logged for Miller's aircraft.

Stukeley Hall in Huntingdonshire which, was used by the Americans during the second world war as Staff Officers' Quarters. This picture taken 15 March 1943. It was at Stukeley Hall where Miller, Baesell, Morgan and Haynes, made their plans. And it was here where General Goodrich was told the part he would play. And, what he had to do.

Wright has his Service Record Card and copy of his orders. So What?

Has Wright got a copy of his Flight Plan? - The answer, No.

And cleared from Beauvais France and Bordeaux - Bordeaux? That is South.

What the hell was he going to Bordeaux for? We see that soon.

And the correct listing is Beauvais/Tille, a pre-war airfield used by the French Air Force. But what has that got to do with it?

And those photocopies Wright sent. How the hell could anybody be so damn cuckoo. Only the Yanks. For the benefit of my Readers I will quote: 'During the investigation of the area of Bordeaux, a search was made for the mentioned deceased, and it was found that there is no trace of them in the area of Bordeaux. - What bunkum! Bordeaux is around 320 miles south of Paris!

So after a good laugh I file them away where they belong - in the bin.

Miller's aircraft spotted by a woman in Royal Observer Corps?

I thought it was foggy?

And radar not working?

Thank goodness this lone sole was on duty - I expect Miller waved to her or, gave her a tune as he flew past, just to make sure she knew it was him ... The vain devil.

5. Now states found the Norseman six miles west of Le Touquet. The plot thickens.

But I thought it was Bordeaux? I expect he had just popped there for a couple of bottles of wine - a sort of early Beaujolais run but, this from Bordeaux. Pity never caught on.

And claims to have found Miller's aircraft. Good Boy. Now show me ... And the world, where it is. Not possible unless where I say.

6. Well!

Not interested what Wright's three cowboys tell him. Miller's aircraft landed and took off (as stated in my Ghost Stations IV) from RAF Twinwood Farm on 15 December 1944.

Wright and his three cowboys should let Miller's son-in-law, Barry Soper, in on the news for he has recently been to England to try and purchase the dilapidated control tower at Twinwood Farm Airfield because he wants to dismantle it - brick-by-brick and ship it 4,000 miles back to Iowa where he is setting up a Miller museum.

And would you believe it - he does not know Miller never used the airfield - shame on Wright for not telling Barry Soper.

7. Baesell was as stated in my book. And here Wright goes again with Bordeaux. What the hell has Bordeaux got to do with Miller?

Nothing.

What evidence does Wright have? ... A postcard from Miller and Baesell from Bordeaux?

8. I have said all I need to say about LACW Dixon. However, let me just clear one small point. It is not LACW Dixie Clerke, she was then, Leading Aircraftwoman Muriel Dixon of the Womens Auxiliary Air Force. Later Mrs Muriel 'Dixie' Clerke who settled in British Columbia. Her story much more than just being confused. Complete fabrication.

And here Wright admits Morgan, Miller, Baesell and Haynes - together.

But then says no mention of Haynes anywhere.

Confucius says ...

And Wright has an interview tape Dixon made in 1983 ... I have a copy of a 1914 Comic Cuts ... that made me laugh also.

9. The Twinwood Farm Airfield was **NOT** closed 15 December 1944. The facts are as in my Ghost Stations. And Honington was Station 375 ... Not 595. RAF Heston briefly housed the American 27th Air Transport Group.

10. The secret tunnels are as stated. Security was my job.

And Wright is a security risk asking questions with people who worked at the R.A.E. They have all signed the Official Secrets Act - so let me have their names.

11. Of course there is no evidence of any kind to support the Podington story - They did not publish it in Standing Orders.

Lack solid documentary evidence Wright says. What a stupid remark. I wrote most of the so-called documentary evidence during the 'fifties.

The documentary trail does not always tell you the Truth - It tells you what those who wrote it - Want you to know.

12. You could say the same for Kennedy.

13. The Burial Files. If open for all as Wright says - Why did he have to appeal to President Reagan for help to see them? What have they got to hide - apart from a body or two.

And here again on about documentary evidence but Wright admits Hess was an imposter by mutual four-power agreement. Well documented, of course by the four-powers? They all **signed** to say what they were doing!

Now, come come. They must have done. Afraid not - Secret devils!

And I was deeply offended by the attack against Wing Commander Reg Stidolph. He was **not** a glory-hunter prepared to 'invent outlandish stories'.

Wing Commander Reg Stidolph - centre, flat cap - with his Flight Commanders and crew at RAF Skellingthorpe where, he was Commanding Officer of No: 61 Squadron

An apology has been demanded - and will be shown in the first available reprint.

Wing Commander Stidolph was Commanding Officer of No 61 Squadron during the second world war, he did not fly a desk - he flew a four-engined Lancaster bomber. It was Wing Commander Reg Stidolph who put Bill Reid forward for his Victoria Cross. And Bill Reid is still around. I saw his picture in the Daily Mail on 1st June 1992.

Let me just give a little background to Wing Commander Stidolph - What sort of man was he?

Since the outbreak of the second world war Stidolph had served in all the main theatres from England to the Far East.

He came to England from Rhodesia in 1935 and joined the Royal Air Force.In 1937 he went to the Fleet Air Arm, specializing in torpedo work with seaplanes until early 1939.

In November 1940, he was controller of flying boats on Suda Bay, Crete and, in March 1941 he found himself in Egypt as Flight Commander in a squadron of Blenheim fighter bombers and carried out eleven operations in the Western Desert.

The following August he took command of the squadron with the rank of Wing Commander.

In December 1941, after being blasted to pieces by German bombers, the squadron was sent back to Delta to re-equip. Within a week it set out for Burma, arrived in Rangoon on 5 January 1942 and, began operations against the Japanese.

After the evacuation of Burma, Stidolph returned to India where he commanded a very advanced RAF base.

Wing Commander Stidolph - second left, seated, as looking at picture - at Senior Officers' Course at RAF Cranwell. A HIGHLY respected officer.

Then back to England but, not before a flight to China. His worst experience was being bombed at Jarabub Oasis, where they lived among gullies and wadis. Though most of the aircrew escaped injury, 35 ground crew were killed.

After being in command of No 61 Squadron at Skellingthorpe in Lincolnshire for three months he had by this time completed more than 50 operations which, included 19 in Blenheims in the Western Desert and 17 in Burma.

And it was Wing Commander Stidolph who gave the Gaumont News interview after the Berlin raid.

Wing Commander Stidolph was awarded the Distinguished Flying Cross. His uncle, Major R.C. Nesbitt won the Victoria Cross in the Mashone rising in 1893, when he was in the Rhodesian Pioneer Column. Stidolph was a true Rhodesian.

This then, the background to Wing Commander Reg Stidolph - a gentleman and, not as Wright slurred, a glory-hunter. Wright speaks of himself.

14. This was the best piece of waffle I have ever read. Now Wright says Miller flew to Paris on 14 December 1944 and on the Saturday, 16th, played at a big party at SHAEF.

And his source, an LACW was at the party - hobnobbing I expect with all the Top Brass and telling them how to win the war!

And Wright claims Miller chatted with this LACW Joan Heath - driver to Air Chief Marshal Sir Arthur Tedder - and Miller told her he was going Stateside for a few days over Christmas and **she** agreed to take him to Buc Airfield.

It just shows ... If you want to get a top job done, ask the daily cleaner. How bloody far-fetched can you get.

But that is not the end of it. The Bobcat aircraft was lost - They were going back to Bordeaux for more wine, by the way - the wreck and bodies were sighted in June 1946 from the air - but not found. How sad. How very, very, sad.

But there is more. The Top Brass at SHAEF, that is short for Supreme Headquarters Allied Expeditionary Force had no idea of Miller's fate ... Just a moment while I dry my eyes from laughing ... and because Miller's Christmas Day broadcast was imminent they - the Top Brass, fabricated the Norseman story with the help of Haynes. (The man not mentioned in documents).

Now that is a good one.

Oh, and because Miller was AWOL - absent without leave - it was hushed-up.

So where is the documentary evidence which Wright claims so important?

None.

Fact. Miller would not lower himself to speak to a driver ... a driver, an LACW. Not Miller, he was arrogant and not liked, not even by most of his band.

Miller was at the top of the tree and he only had to ask for what he needed ... and he would have got it. Asking an LACW driver, my ass.

15. Now Wright claims Miller's body found. I expect laid out, tunic pressed, buttons shining with a note saying - Miller's body - please find me now!'

Now it is not the driver this time, nor the window cleaner, nor the butcher, nor the baker, nor the candlestick maker ... but the (later) president of United States himself - General Dwight D. Eisenhower, the Supreme Commander who arranged the cover-up.

Cover-up?

What about documentary evidence?

Wright does **NOT** repeat **NOT** know where Miller is buried.

Then Wright says Hess an imposter.

What about all the important documentary evidence? On Hess I have covered in this book.

And my anti-British comments?

I served - Security for Suez, my three brothers in the D-Day Landings, My father (Canadian) fought in the first world war and was at Vimy Ridge, my Uncle George in both the first and second world wars - Anti-British? The British government has done sod-all for those who fought and gave their all.

Just ask any British war pensioner and, if that is anti-British for speaking the truth - Then I am anti-British.

Let us remember, it was the British who -

Set up the first prisoner-of-war camp. That was during the Napoleonic war and from its few thousand inmates, only a handful survived. Set up the first concentration-camp during the Boar War. It was **NOT** the Germans. It was the British.

And at time of writing we have the Matrix Churchill affair - and as three innocent men take the rap, the British government .... 'No Lies, honest!'

Need I say more?

Oh! Napoleon was killed by the British.

So my proof comes from many sources - the main being Wing Commander Stidolph and Mrs Betty Hockey who **SAW** Major Glenn Miller in March 1945. Her signed proof is on page 16 of my Ghost Stations IV.

And I would take the word of Wing Commander Stidolph and Betty Hockey against all the Top Brass and Wilbur Wright's in the world.

The Miller story is as told in my Ghost Stations ... Factual to the last dot.

IS THERE A PARALLEL DIMENSION?

Stranger than Fiction. Let me tell you a story which might give you much more than food for thought but, leave you in no doubt that there is a parallel dimension.

In March 1975 Dick 'Dickie' Smith was setting out for Ostend in his light aircraft and, was just near Chelmsford when he picked up a faint message ... he could not believe it. As a former wartime bomber pilot, Dickie knew it was an S.O.S. from a crew about to ditch.

The message was very faint but Dickie was able to establish it was from Halifax LL413 and sounded like May-Day for aircraft going down. 'I tried to trace the message but it only got fainter, then suddenly it was gone,' said Dickie.

So what was the ghostly message? I researched and found that a four-engined Halifax bomber, number LL413, from No 297 Squadron did in fact fail-to-return from an air sea rescue search over the North Sea on 3 March 1945. It just vanished without trace.

But how could Dickie Smith pick up a message three decades later ...? That was a mystery and one that I could not answer. It was clearly the last message he heard from the aircraft. From what I could find out it just disappeared in 1945 and was never found.

A mystery. Then three decades later an even bigger mystery.

But that is not the first time such messages from the past have been received. Alan Holmes, a radio officer on the QE2, said he received a message from the liner, Queen Mary.

Nothing strange about that, you might say. But it was strange - very strange for at the time he received the message the Queen Mary was no longer in service as a liner. She had been turned into a conference centre at Long Beach harbour in California.

Could it have been a hoax?

Not possible. The message was in a code procedure which was no longer used. Holmes recognized it immediately as a routine position check being transmitted from the Queen Mary liner to Portishead Radio at Burnham in Somerset.

So what is the explanation?

The answer that Alan Holmes gave might also explain the ghostly message that Dickie Smith received. He said, 'The signal had bounced out into space and just zipped around until it found its way back to Earth.'

A very logical answer. In fact, no one can come up with a better explanation. But you could put forward a Parallel Dimension as a theory.

Radio is a very new invention and the messages are still winging their way through space. Then, out there in space ... they might be received and inform those receiving same that there is life on another planet.

Remember, one light-year is about ten million, million kilometres. And to give you an example, the star Vega, is a mere twenty-six light-years away from the sun. Vega is one of the three bright stars that dominate the western sky during the early winter months. It can be seen very clearly in the early evening.

THE GHOST OF BLUE BELL HILL

In September 1933, Rochester Council purchased 105 acres of land between the Rochester-Maidstone and Chatham roads for the purpose of developing a municipal airport. Short Bros. who, had been in the area since 1913, then leased the land.

By the end of 1934 other firms had moved into Rochester and, air services were established on 9 June 1934 when Short's began a service from Rochester to Southend.

It is interesting to note - in todays world of women in this and, women in that at fever pitch - that in 1934 a small hangar was built for a private aircraft owner-pilot ... a Miss G. Batcheler, the first woman in the country to have a pilot's licence. And done without burning her bra.

In 1938 the RAF formed No. 23 Elementary and Reserve Flying School at Rochester. A second hangar was built in July 1938 when the school was expanded to train pilots for the Fleet Air Arm.

During 1939 the factory was extended and the mighty four-engined Stirling bomber started to be produced at Rochester. This made Rochester a main Luftwaffe target and, on 15 August 1940, the airfield was attacked by enemy aircraft, resulting in severe damage to Short's factory and the destruction of six Stirlings on the production line.

On the night of the air raid, a young lady set out from Maidstone, to cycle back to Rochester, to see her boyfriend who worked at Rochester airfield. Just before she reached Blue Bell Hill, her chain broke. In desperation to get to

Rochester she ran out to stop a lorry but, on the wartime dipped lights, the driver did not see her and she received a glancing blow - knocking her to the ground and, it was alleged she fell under the back wheels of the lorry.

A few months after the accident a person reported running over a young lady at Blue Bell Hill but, when he got out to offer help ... she had vanished.

Over the years dozens of people have reported running over a young lady ... only to find it is the Ghost of Blue Bell Hill.

THE OSSINGTON MYSTERY

About a year after reading The Unseen Servant story in my Ghost Stations III, Ken Billingham, the son of Sergeant Walter Billingham featured in the story, visited the old Ossington airfield. Ken takes up the story:

'I recently paid a visit to the remains of RAF Ossington and, I soon became aware of a strange atmosphere in the vicinity of the Northwood, where the remains of some of the old huts and buildings still exist, covered in undergrowth and trees. The drive up to the site of the hall seems very foreboding and still. I didn't notice any birds singing, the old chapel is still there and still used. But it has a sad and gloomy atmosphere about it. I can well imagine My dad having to walk up that drive in the dark of the winter nights of November 1941.'

The main gates to what was once Ossington Hall ... now only the ghost of Viscountess Ossington remains. (B)

During his visit Ken found the bases of two hangars and, to the west of the northwood the old MT Section that is still used by the farmer for storage. He experienced a very eerie, sad atmosphere about the old airfield.

And, that was very much so on the site of Ossington Hall which, was demolished in 1963 because no one wanted to live in it - The last owners of the Hall being the Viscount and Viscountess Ossington - whose family name was Denison.

And they hold the key to the 'unseen force' that Sergeant Billingham and, many other airmen experienced that November night in 1941 when billeted in Ossington Hall. 'There was an 'Evil' presence in the room,' said Sergeant Billingham.

And demolishing the hall did not remove the eerie, supernatural atmosphere. One night in 1981 the local game-keeper and two friends were out on patrol.

View of Ossington Hall from the lake.

Map of Ossington

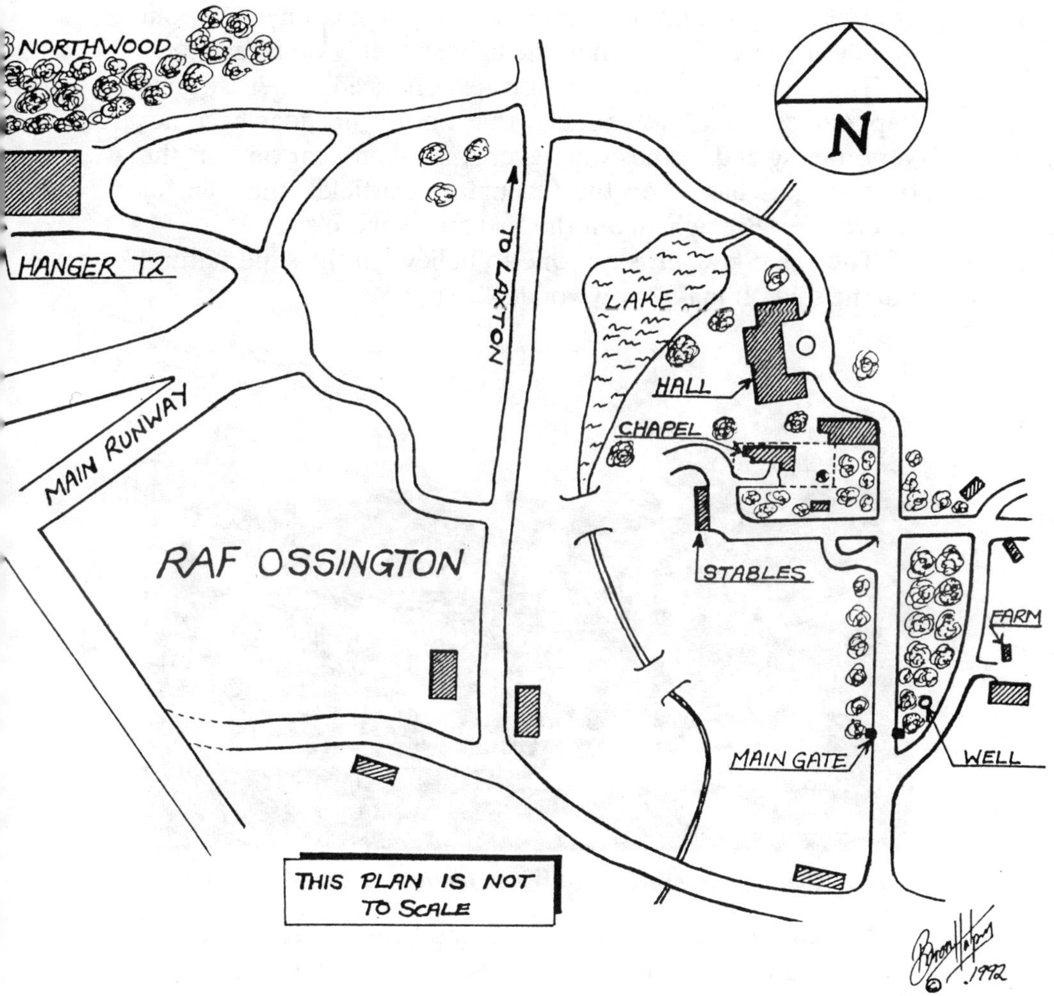

They parked their van on the site of the hall and were just sitting there ... when suddenly ... the van was enveloped in a very bright light.

They immediately thought that someone had come up the drive behind them with headlights on full. But when they got out there was no one there, nor any sign of anyone about ... only an eerie silence when the light suddenly vanished!

The game-keeper has also experienced other strange happenings. He has noticed that one of his dogs becomes very uneasy and whines whenever it is taken near one of the old hangar bases on the Ossington Airfield, the hangar where Ken Billingham felt the 'sad atmosphere'.

The game-keeper is not one to believe in the supernatural but, he said, 'It makes you wonder.'

Ossington Hall showing North Wing - on right as looking at picture.

It is all very strange. And the game-keeper then said about the strange happenings at the Ossington Hotel in Newark. This was built by Viscountess Ossington as a temporance hotel in 1881.

It appears that some very strange things have been going on there over the years, since the hotel began selling alcohol ... Bottles of wines and spirits have mysteriously moved around. Doors on the top floor - where the Viscountess Ossington had a bedroom - refused to open when they were unlocked. The doors would be held shut by an 'Unseen Force', then suddenly open. The picture of Viscountess Ossington would remove itself from the wall, even though the hook on the wall was still in place ... The picture was always found on the floor near her bedroom ... moved by an 'Unseen Force'. But, as the 'Unseen Force' was none other than the Spirit of Viscountess Ossington, the picture was never damaged.

But the 'Unseen Force' does use an evil force as Sergeant Billingham felt. It is alleged that an electrician working on the flood-lighting at the Ossington Hotel, claimed he was pushed off his ladder ... By an 'Unseen Force'!

The Ossington Hotel, Newark. Closed down when picture taken January 1992. (C)

And remember ... It was an 'Unseen Force' that Sergeant Billingham experienced at Ossington Hall in November 1941.

Was it the same 'Unseen Force'? Was the 'Unseen Servant' in my story (page 63 Ghost Stations III), none other than the 'Unseen Viscountess Ossington'? The answer is certainly, yes.

At the Ossington Hotel the strange happenings only started after it started selling alcohol. At Ossington Hall, Sergeant Billingham thought that the reason he had been spared from that evil unseen force, was because he was unarmed.

But what about the mysterious light that the game-keeper experienced?

Could it have been the 'Unseen Viscountess' behind the light that enveloped the game-keepers van?

And here again, the answer is, Yes. But what is the connection, you may well ask? The connection is clear. The Ossington game-keeper was formerly employed on the Welbeck Estate. And whilst working there, he was hit by an 'Unseen Force'. 'It was as if someone had hit me in the back with a plank of wood,' he said. Yet he was alone ... nothing or no one was seen.

But what is the connection with Viscountess Ossington and Welbeck Abbey, you may ask? To find out, let us retrace our steps to the main gate of Ossington Hall.

Close to the main gate you will find an ornamental well - erected by Viscountess Ossington in October 1877, to the memory of Edward Denison, son of Edward, Bishop of Salisbury, born 8 September 1840 and died at Melbourne 26 January 1870.

John Evelyn Denison was created 'Viscount Ossington' on 13 February, 1872, but died, at Ossington Hall on 7 March 1873. The peerage then became extinct. He was buried at the Ossington Chapel cemetery on 13 March 1873, where he remains to this day. He was born at Ossington Hall on 27 January 1800, the son of John Denison (formerly Wilkinson), M.P. of Ossington and, his second wife Charlotte. He was educated at Eton and Oxford. Became Member of Parliament for Newcastle-U-Lyme 1823-26 and, was in politics until 1872.

He was speaker of the House of Commons 1857. On 14 July 1827 he married at All Souls, just off Portland Place, to Charlotte, Third daughter of William Henry (Cavendish-Scott-Bentinck) Fourth Duke of Portland - she was born 14 January 1806. After the death of her husband, she became on the death of her brother, the Fifth Duke of Portland - William John Cavendish-Scott-Bentinck - on 6 December 1879, co-heirship with sister Lucy, Baroness de Walden.

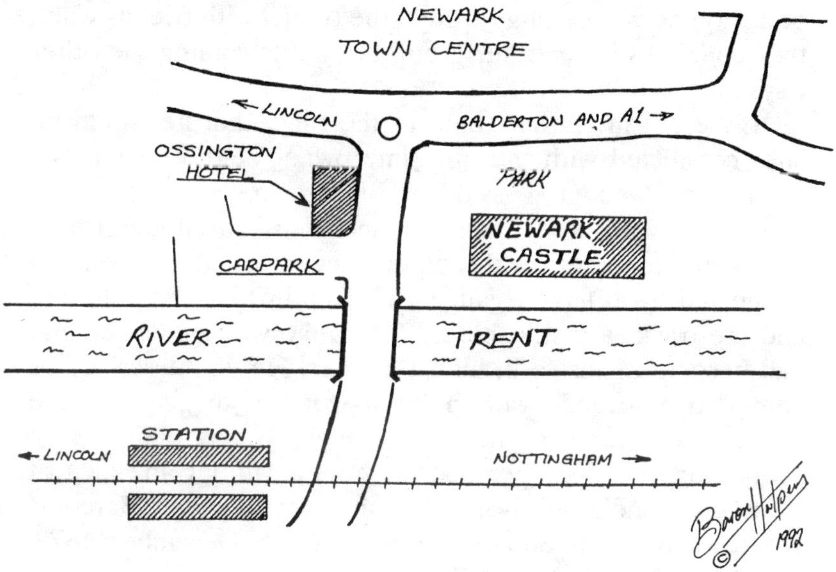

Map of Newark showing the haunted Ossington Hotel.

Now I trust you are beginning to see the connection. But there is more ... much more.

A considerable part of the family estates included Portland Place in London and 8,247 acres in Ayrshire.

On 26 June 1882, she took, by royal licence, the name Scott in lieu of Denison. She died at Ossington Hall on 30 September 1889 in her 84th year.

It is interesting to note that her brother the Fifth Duke of Portland, was responsible for the extensive underground excavation at Welbeck Abbey during the mid-nineteenth century.

The works consisted of a series of tunnels complete with skylights. The main tunnel was large enough to take a coach and horses and, actually passed under the lake to the south lodge.

In the nineteen-thirties Walter Billingham - the same Sergeant Walter Billingham posted to RAF Ossington in 1941 - cycled through the main tunnel many times. On one occassion he was cycling through the tunnel with friends when they collided with another group of cyclists coming the other way.

'Little did my father think at the time, that he would be later connected with the one time owner of those tunnels - Viscountess Ossington,' said Ken Billingham.

Other works at Welbeck included an underground ballroom, together with other underground rooms, all connected by a narrow gauge electric railway. The ballroom and the tracks are still there. The Duke was unmarried and had become reclusive in his later years. He was described as being 'so absorbed', with his vast work of digging out the underground tunnels and rooms, that he was oblivious of everything else. He persued his hobby without any idea of beauty, a lonely self-isolated man. He died at Harcourt House, Cavendish Square, London, on 6 December 1879, aged 79, and was buried at Kensal Green cemetery.

And as a matter of interest, let me just mention another curious story concerning the eccentric Duke. This happened seventeen years after his death and became known as the 'Druce Case'.

In 1896, the widow of Walter Thomas Druce made an application to the Home Secretary for the opening of a coffin in the Druce family vault in Highgate cemetery.

She alleged that T.C. Druce was in fact the Fifth Duke of Portland, who, after playing for some years at being an upholsterer, had staged a sham death and burial of himself as

'Druce' in 1864 and, that the coffin which was supposed to contain his body was empty.

Mrs Druce retired from the case in 1903 to enter a mental home but, other members of the family continued to contest for the Portland millions.

A company was formed with a capital of over £30,000, subscribed by the public in expectation of receiving enormous profits. Eleven years after Mrs Druce began the case, the coffin was opened.

And inside ...? The body of T.C. Druce.

At the time of writing the Ossington Hotel in Newark is closed ... the bar carpet sporting a thick layer of white fungus.

The tunnel, through which Walter Billingham cycled is still there but closed to the public. Indeed, all the tunnels are still there and, could hold many secrets. During the second world war such places were used to safeguard items of high value.

Only recently we had the story of the unsolved mystery of the Illingworth gold bullion. Lady Illingworth - who died a virtual pauper in a council nursing home in 1986 - had claimed the ingots had been placed in vaults at the National Westminster Bank. The bank insisted it never had any of the Illingworth gold - and doubted it had ever existed.

So where is the 'missing' bullion? We do know that Lord Illingworth did not like Winston Churchill and the way he was conducting the war. It is thought that Lord Illingworth collected the gold bullion for safe keeping at the outset of the second world war. It was a fact that the tide of war was flowing with Germany in the early years. Thus, a network of tunnels such as at Welbeck Abbey would make a very secure and ideal place to store items of value. Hidden away and the tunnel sealed - the Italians did it with their wine - it would be safe for ever and a day. The secret safe - the trouble is, Lord Illingworth died in 1942.

It was just a theory anyway. But one that could be true. Welbeck Abbey in Nottinghamshire was a long way from the planned German invasion. And Lord Illingworth was a

Yorkshireman ... Just a thought ... a sealed tunnel with all those secrets ...

And all this from just retracing our steps to the main gate of Ossington Hall!

A haunting scene ... the chapel clock tower at Ossington. (A)

THE MYSTERIOUS RUDOLF HESS

The more you think about Deputy Fuhrer Rudolf Hess - the mystery deepens. In my Ghost Station IV book - The White Flag ... And Hess - I said that the ghost of Hess will haunt the Allies.

But since writing that book new information is to hand. Returning from Italy to England I went via Germany and stayed a few days with my good friend Ulrich. He took me for the usual night out and introduced me to a former Luftwaffe pilot. And, throughout the evening, I not only digested the Wiener Schnitzel but, also, what he told me about Hess. And, it has made me look again at the facts that we have to hand.

The former Luftwaffe pilot said that the whole story was fabricated by the British Intelligence. Adolf Hitler had been informed of the plan right from the start. By now Hess had served his purpose and his aircraft was intercepted and shot down, possibly either by Oberstleutnant Heinz Bar or Oberst Werner Molders.

So let us go over the facts again. It does appear that the British were expecting someone special to drop in during the early months of 1941.

Looking at the photographs of the wreckage of the mysterious Rudolf Hess's Messerschmidt 110 long-range fighter - this by the way was not an aircraft for fools, its fuel system was very complicated and wide open to mis-use, as with most German aircraft - you will see that the cockpit section is missing. Why?

And why was RAF Intelligence in such a tearing hurry to remove the wreckage from Number 63 Maintenance Unit?

The cockpit section is still **supposed** - repeat, **supposed**, to be kept under lock and key by the RAF somewhere!

What was so special about the cockpit?

Was it fitted with **dual** controls?

Was it flown to Scotland by someone else who went to ground after bailing out?

The so-called 'Hess' could have bailed out of a British aircraft, or, someone else could have bailed out and the mysterious Hess could have arrived on the scene. The whole operation could have been made to look like a home-guard exercise!

And that is what did happen.

The wreckage of the mysterious Hess does not look as if it has just crashed. It does not look 'fresh'. Remember, it was supposed to be a **new** aircraft, yet this wreckage looks as if it has been lying around a scrapyard for months.

To study the photographs of the wreckage you will notice that the fabric covering of the rudders and elevators is missing. It is stripped clean.

Could army souvenir hunters have done this when there were lots of cotton bits and pieces to pick up?

A small fire was reported. But not near the tail section. And I failed to notice a swastika on the fins of the mysterious Hess's aircraft.

None of it adds up and I must now certainly agree with Hugh Thomas and his book, 'Hess, A Tale of Two Murders.' The mysterious Hess was an imposter.

Let us look at the flying kit of the mysterious Hess. Surely, that must be straight forward. But no, here the mystery only deepens.

For a start. A Mae-West life jacket is conspicuous by its absence!

A Mae-West is a must for over water flying. And the flight-path for the mysterious Hess was over an awful lot of water.

A picture taken on 9 October 1945 when the mysterious Hess was being interrogated by Colonel John Amen at Nuremburg, shows the mysterious Hess in some of his flying kit.

Yet an official statement said that the flying kit and all the mysterious Hess's personal belongings had been destroyed.

As former president Bush would say - 'Read my Lips.'

In December 1988 it was made known that the mysterious Hess's flying kit and other items were coming up for auction!

But lo and behold ... the sale had to be cancelled. Why? They were stolen and a British officer at Spandau prison was charged with theft and extortion.

How very, very strange.

The whole story surrounding Deputy Fuhrer Hess was a fake. A sham that has fooled the world to this day.

The wreckage was put there to add credibility to the story. The bits could have come from other Messerschmidt 110's. And the radio call sign on the fuselage VJ+OQ could have been painted on or, even altered.

And to make everyone think that it was Deputy Fuhrer Rudolf Hess, a story was leaked about three SS Parachutists who were supposed to have arrived to **murder** Hess.

This was another fabrication.

The files just recently released on Hess told you nothing which, proves he was an imposter. The files now on view to the public are letters supposed to have been written by Hess about his food being poisoned.

The more you read ... the more it smells like a cover-up.

It is said Hess kept trying to commit suicide. If that was so - why bother to write saying the food is poisoned.

And the final touch - Goodbye letters to Hitler, his wife and children.

Very touching but not at all convincing.

But by solving that the Deputy Fuhrer Rudolf Hess was an imposter ... It creates an even bigger mystery.

Who was the mysterious Hess ...?

And why ...?

THE MYTHICAL 88

This is not as such a ghost story but in a way, the mythical 88 played a major role in creating the Ghost Squadrons that today haunt the old airfields.

In its primary role, the 88mm flak gun took a heavy toll of Allied bombers during the early war years ... they were easy prey for the mighty 88.

It did not take long for the 88 to gain a fearful reputation and respect from the Allied forces. One of war cartoonist Biss Mauldin's 'Willie and Joe' cartoons, showed two American GI's, very dishevelled, talking with a GI sitting at a make shift desk, on which, was pinned a sign - Prisoner of War Interrogator. The cartoon caption said: 'I'll let ya know if I find th' one wot invented the 88.'

So what was the mythical 88? To find out we must go back before the war started ... and as we dig ... a mystery unfolds.

The mighty 88 was designed in the 1920s and, it was Adolf Hitler - who, having fought in the first world war, saw its potential - authorized full scale manufacture of the anti-aircraft gun and, it first saw action in 1939. The 88 had an effective ceiling of 34,770 feet.

That was fantastic but, its main claim to fame was in the role as an anti-tank gun. And in that role it was used by Field Marshal Erwin Rommel's Afrika Korps to great effect in North Africa, particularly at Sollum, Halfaya and El Alamein.

But that was not all - the first heavy German tank, the Tiger, was equipped with the tank version of Germany's most powerful anti-tank gun - the mighty 88mm KwK (L/56).

The Mythical 88 in its primary role. An 88mm flak battery in one of its quieter moments. October 1943.

Thus it was deadly to tangle with a Tiger and, when introduced in 1942 it was the world's most powerful and heavily armed tank. The Tiger tank became a legend. Its 88mm gun had a killing range of just under 10 miles.

In July 1944 during the battle of the Falaise Gap in Normandy, a lone Tiger tank blocked the advance of the British 7th Armoured Division and blasted to kingdom come twenty-five armoured vehicles in the process ... all felled by the Tiger's mighty 88.

No wonder then, that the mighty 88 was regarded as a wonder weapon with almost mythical powers.

And building on those mythical powers, the Germans mounted the formidable 88 anti-aircraft gun upon a Panther tank chassis, to create the auf Panzerjager Panther but Hitler renamed it the Jagdpanther, tank destroyer.

The Jagdpanther appeared on the battle-field in October 1943 and served - with devastating effect - with the Wehrmacht anti-tank battalions. The mighty 88 making mince-meat of all in its path.

But why did the Allies let the 88 become such a forceful weapon?

That is the mystery for the British had an equivalent weapon in the 94mm (3.7 inch) anti-aircraft gun. And, those who handled the British gun knew it was much more than just an anti-aircraft gun ... it was also a deadly anti-tank gun.

But for some unknown reason the British weapon was never used in the role as an anti-tank weapon or, fitted to any British tanks.

Another of the second world war's little mysteries.

UFO

UFO - OVER HAROLD HILL

And Derek Smith also had a close encounter with a UFO. President Ronald Reagan and his wife Nancy, both were adamant that they had seen a flying saucer.

In one incident in 1990, the Belgian Air Force scrambled two jet fighters to intercept a UFO. But when the pilots returned, they were forbidden to talk about it. The airforce did admit they found nothing, yet they still threw a veil of secrecy over the whole operation. Very strange and sinister.

The UFO was reported to be triangular in shape with three bright lights and, as the two jets approached, it appeared to black itself out and disappeared yet was still on radar - then with incredible acceleration - it was gone.

It was a similar story from Derek Smith:

'In the autumn of 1980, I was on the night shift, patrolling in a police car, around the Harold Hill estate, about 2.30 a.m. - 3 a.m. I stopped the car, and parked in Bridgewater Road near the junction with Hilldene Close, at the rear of the library. I turned out the car lights and settled into my seat to have a cigarette.

'I had been parked for about ten or fifteen minutes and, was thinking of resuming patrol, when I suddenly saw a brilliant ball of electric blue light, appear over the top of my windscreen. It appeared to be the size of a tennis ball and, was about ten or fifteen feet in the air. It suddenly accelerated into movement, very fast, along Bridgewater Road, swerved left behind the library, (into Hilldene Close) and went out of my sight.

'I started the car and drove after it but it had vanished. I drove around the area looking and debating with myself, about what I had seen and whether to tell anybody but, I decided to keep it to myself.

'The night was dry and warm, there were no thunderstorms or rain that night. And as the car was stationary with the engine turned off, there is no way that the light was a street light reflection caused by the movement of the car.'

UFO - OVER BILLINGSHURST

Alan Waddington is very down-to-earth and, the last person that I would expect, to try and invent a flying saucer story.

'As a person I am interested in aviation and have lived near to municipal and service airfields,' he said. 'I have never come across such intense lights on conventional aircraft at night time, though I took them initially to be landing lights. However this theory was smashed by the realisation that the same pattern of lights was seen when the 'aircraft' was flying away from me. Although another aircraft was visible and audible in the vicinity of my position the other craft made no audible sound either in approach or in passing.

'It then appeared to 'hover' above the rooftops (my horizon) though at some distance beyond Billingshurst, and we then thought that it might be a helicopter though again there was none of the sound that identifies a conventional helicopter, in approach or flypast.

'The white lights appeared to be much brighter than the white sodium lighting in the streets. The following night I heard a light aircraft fly over Billingshurst and observed that it had one white flashing light under the fuselage. The light was not so intense as that seen the previous night which obscured the craft's shape and, the wingtip lights were also visible.

'The light aircraft flew from east to west and was obvious as an aircraft. I do not feel that we misjudged the one with another.'

The following is the report that Alan Waddington made out after sighting the UFO.

REPORT OF AN UNIDENTIFIED FLYING OBJECT

1. Date, time and duration of sightings

   Monday, 1st October 1979 - 19.40 hrs, approx 10 mins.

2. A description, including, shape, size, colour and brightness of the object and whether it made any noise:

   my attention was drawn to three silvery white rotating lights in the night sky, the middle one surmounted by a steady red light, approaching over nearby house rooftops. No apparent sound.

3. Your position at the time geographically:

   Billingshurst, West Sussex 084257 (OS sheet 197)

4. Whether you saw the object with the naked eye, binoculars etc, and whether you succeeded in photographing it:

   initially seen with the naked eye, but by the time I had got my binoculars from the car, it had passed 'over' the house. I observed it for a few moments by the garage, returning to the house. The binoculars did not provided much more detail than I, my wife and eldest daughter observed from the house. No photographs (sketch).

5. The direction in which the UFO was first seen:

   From the north-west heading eastwards at approx 135 degrees.

6. Angle of sight:

   initially at approx 50 degrees having passed over house approx 75 degrees

7. Distance away (with landmarks for reference):

   when seen initially aircraft was climbing behind object. Gatwick airport estimate that the aircraft would be at approx 3000/4000 feet. The aircraft navigation lights were conventional and totally different from UFO, which was lower in sky than aircraft.

8. What movements the object made with speed estimates:

   initially object flew straight course at a slow speed

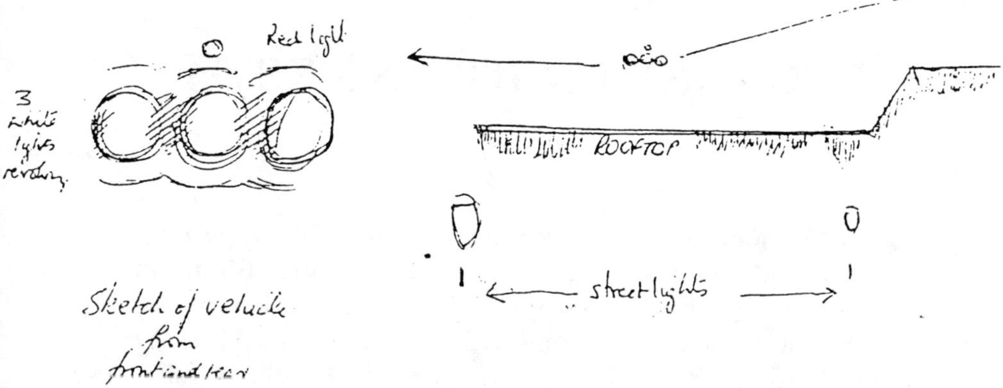

Sketch of UFO as drawn by Alan Waddington just after he saw it.

akin to that of aircraft making a landing approach. It then appeared to hover over the tops of houses to the rear of ours for some time. Our house is lower on the hillside than those, so that if in conventional flight it would have disappeared behind them over the 'crest' of the hill. Having maintained station for some five minutes, it then moved off in a north-easterly direction, disappearing from view behind trees and other roofs. It would be difficult to estimate speeds, without point of reference. The object looked the same from the rear as it did on approach.

9. Weather conditions:

   Bright clear sky, stars visible, moon visible, to S, little to no cloud.

10. Nearby objects on ground:

    Only houses as mentioned

11. Notified police or other authorities;

    Duty Officer, Gatwick Airport (2nd Oct).

UFO - AND LIGHTNING XS894

At 2200 hours on Tuesday 8 September 1970, Lightning XS894 lifted off the runway at Royal Air Force Binbrook and climbed quickly into the night sky over Lincolnshire.

The story of the Lightning XS894 mystery is told in my Ghost Stations Book Two ... the full story ... well, as full a story as permitted to say at the time. But now the truth about Lightning XS894 can be told.

A 5 Squadron Lightning as flown by Captain Schafner.

In Ghost Stations Two (page 197) I do say that in 1987, seventeen years after the incident, I set about trying to solve the eerie mystery ... having served in the Royal Air Force Special Security I could open doors others were not able to do. But, even I could not chip away the veil of secrecy that surrounded the Lightning mystery. At the Ministry of Defence ... doors were closed in my face. At the all-telling United States Air Force Records Office ... I only had to mention Captain Schafner and Lightning XS894 to have the door slammed in my face. Sealed lips.

And all of this only added to the mystery which, made me all the more determined to solve the Lightning mystery.

Many of you will have read the Lightning XS894 mystery in my Ghost Stations Book Two but, for the benefit of those who have not read my books and, not familiar with the story, I will go back for the purpose of giving it briefly from the beginning.

The QRA - Quick Reaction Alert shelter that housed two Lightning fighters on 24-hour readiness. It was these Lightnings that should have answered the UFO alert. Not Schafner. So why was he allowed to go on his own? Two aircraft always go.

The single-seater jet fighter took off as stated, at the controls was an American pilot, Captain William Schafner who, was on his second tour at RAF Binbrook. He loved to fly the Lightning and was very well familiar with it.

Just after one hour after getting airborne, Captain Schafner informed Binbrook that he was in trouble.

That is the first clue and will come back to that in a minute.

He went on to say the Lightning was still flyable and on that information Binbrook control ordered him out over the sea to the ditching area ... where he was told to meet up with a Shackleton before ditching.

As soon as he was over the ditching area Captain Schafner was told to eject --- the normal procedure ... but he did not do so.

As the valuable seconds ticked away the Shackleton circled the area. The crew being at a loss as to why he did not eject.

Suddenly the Lightning went slowly down and settled on the sea like a great metal bird.

The Shackleton appeared overhead and illuminated the area ... they wanted to give the pilot all the help possible. They were relieved to see the pilot climb out onto the wing and get into the sea ... But did the crew see him get out? They thought they did and at the time they said they saw him climb out onto the wing.

The Lightning floated on the sea ... then slowly ... it sank beneath the waves ... and settled on the sea bed in an upright position.

Back at RAF Binbrook, Captain Schafner's wife was told her husband had to ditch in the sea just off Flamborough Head but, not to worry for the Shackleton was with him and that the crew had seen him get out before the aircraft went down.

The first part of the cover up had begun.

Despite an extensive search by the Air Sea Rescue ... Captain Schafner could not be found.

The Ministry of Defence then added: 'I don't think he got out of the plane, no wreckage was found.'

What a stupid statement. The Lightning went down in one piece ... it did not break up.

Why the sudden change of story after the Shackleton crew said they saw Captain Schafner get out and into the sea ...?

With a so-called investigation underway, the Lightning was recovered from the sea bed. The divers who went down, saw the Lightning sitting on the sea bed ... it was a very eerie sensation ... for the canopy was **STILL** on but the pilot was gone ...!

How had he got out with the canopy still in place?

It was a chilling ... eerie ... mystery.

On examination back at RAF Binbrook it was found that Lightning XS894 had only slight nose damage ... otherwise it was perfect. The cockpit was **closed** and no pilot inside. No one could answer that.

The ejector seat was intact. The mechanism for the ejector seat had fired but not worked ... what is called a 'Light Strike' - it did the strike but did not blow the canopy and the seat was still in place. So very, very strange.

So where was Captain Schafner?

And that was where I left it. Now I can tell the true story and, although cannot answer where Captain Schafner is ... I can explain what happened to him that dark September night in 1970.

So what did happen ...?

On the night in question, Captain Schafner was preparing for a routine flight, when suddenly, the Station got a call to intercept an Unidentified Flying Object - UFO. Lightning XS894 was scrambled to intercept the UFO.

The Lightning was the perfect machine for such a duty. The Lightning was built for the RAF as a supersonic Mach 2 interceptor. From cold start to airborne in ninety seconds, very high rate of climb and phenomenal acceleration. Initial rate of climb being over 8 miles (12 kilometres) a minute - reaching 40,000 feet in 2.5 minutes from brakes off. And it could zoom climb to well over 70,000 feet. Thus, the perfect beast to tackle a UFO and, it was a chance Captain Schafner could not refuse.

RAF Binbrook just after it closed. No 5 Squadron hangar in fore on left. It was from the 5 Squadron crew room that Schafner dashed to his Lightning, just outside the crew room, to the fore of the control tower. A mystery for Schafner should not have answered the alert. But in typical 'Loud Mouth' American style, he did. And paid the price.

Those at RAF Binbrook involved in the mysterious disappearance of Captain Schafner were afraid to talk. But eventually someone did - but under great fear and only on condition that I do not dilvulge their name. I gave my word.

It is alleged, that as the Lightning approached the UFO, an energy beam hit the Lightning and it became under the control of the UFO.

Using aetheric energy the energy beam is able to disintegrate matter and convert it back into free energy. This was how Captain Schafner was removed.

Time stopped. The Lightning helpless and, as if guided by remote control from the UFO, it returned to earth and rested on the sea bed ... minus Captain Schafner whose last radio message was ... 'The lights on the UFO have now blacked out ... do not feel to be in control ...'

So was that the answer ...?

Captain Schafner's body has never been found. And, I am informed that he took off without signing Form 700 which, would never be done ... unless, of course, there was a UFO ... then you would certainly not hang around signing forms.

The Lightning returned to earth ... canopy closed ... ejector seat in place ... the pilot gone!

No: 5 Squadron crew room from where Schafner dashed to his Lightning. Today, silent ... only the ghosts.

UFO - AND THE SWISS HOLES

At the time of the mysterious disappearance of Captain Schafner from Lightning XS894, UFO sightings were made and, mysterious holes suddenly appeared in Switzerland.

But what has this to do with Ghost Stations.you may ask?

There could be a link with Captain Schafner's mysterious disappearance.

Also, let us remember, many UFO sightings have been made over airfields.

It was in 1952 when four airman stationed at RAF Topcliffe in Yorkshire stated that they had seen a mysterious object in the sky. It first appeared above the control tower ... a huge silver disc.

Also, airmen from RAF Topcliffe reported seeing a Meteor Jet Fighter being shadowed by a 'flying saucer' which suddenly accelerated away at ubelievable speed.

And there is still the unexplained UFOs sighted over RAF Lakenheath in 1956. They were identified by radar. One UFO was stationary at about 20,000 feet and as the RAF fighter, scrambled to intercept, the UFO moved behind the fighter. At all times being tracked by ground radar.

The fighter pilot could not 'shake' the mysterious UFO and a second fighter was scrambled. But all contact was suddenly lost.

Just as Captain Schafner in Lightning XS894 reported, 'UFO suddenly blacked out and contact lost' ... But in his case the UFO was still there ...

For the past two years UFOs have been reported over Belgium and, the Belgian Air Force has scrambled F-16 fighters to intercept them on many occasions - the UFOs being clearly seen on radar.

'The Belgian skies have experienced extraordinary phenomena', said Wilfried de Brouwer, Belgium's Air Force Chief of Staff.

The holes in Switzerland are a mystery and were found after a UFO had been sighted. Holes in the earth have also been found in Russia and, with the holes in the earth it is not possible for people to claim that they are made by whirlwinds or helicopters, as with the corn circles - nor can the holes in the earth be hoaxes, as with the corn circles.

The holes in the earth found in Switzerland may have some bearing on the mysterious disappearance of Captain Schafner.

Let me explain. Many people reckon that the Roswell, New Mexico story of a crashed alien space craft being found by the US Airforce and taken to Wright Patterson Army Air Field together with some dead aliens ... where they remain to this day, is absolutely true.

The intelligence officer, Major Jesse Marcel who, was there at the time, actually released the story to the press. Then, of course, the 'balloon-went-up' and a cover story was quickly issued stating that it was only a weather balloon that had crashed.

The media bought this and, so over 40 years of cover ups and disinformation have been the norm. The Establishment have done their utmost to seal the reality of UFO phenomenon away from the public and strangely the scientific community as well.

'This country is experiencing the greatest wave of jingoism that I have seen in my life,' said Tony Benn in the House of Commons on Tuesday 15 January 1991. My good friend Tony Benn was talking about the Gulf War ... The jingoism fell on deaf ears with the nine Gulf War soldiers killed by the Americans so-called 'friendly fire' - A cover up? A government whitewash?

Yes. And it was just the same at Cassino during the second world war when, it was American 'friendly bombing', that killed Allied soldiers. So the government cover-up continues.

The mysterious Swiss holes in the earth are in the area around Lake Geneva.

The first to appear was just two metres in diameter with a depth of one-and-a-half metres.

The hole that appeared at Ollon in May 1981 had a diameter of 5 metres and a depth of 8 metres. Total earth removed being 157 cubic metres.

The recent hole at Conflignon in February 1990 being 10 metres in diameter and 12 metres deep. The volume of earth being removed being 942 cubic metres.

But anyone can dig a hole, you might say. And how do you know they are not hoaxes?

The strange holes in the earth all point to an alien force for the following reasons.

All the holes have displayed unusual features.

The holes are perfectly round circles and there is no trace of any topsoil in any of them and, if it had been a straight case of soil-subsidence, top soil would be on the floor of the hole.

There is no visible trace of foot or vehicle marks, nor of the soil from the hole. The area is clean and unmarked in anyway.

So what is the answer?

Expert investigators have come up with the answer and, say the soil is removed by ... wait for it ... an energy beam from a alien craft. - Captian Schafner was removed from his lightning by an energy beam.

The energy beam cuts the designated hole to the desired depth and the cylinder-shaped 'probe-core' is taken aboard the alien craft by means of an anti-gravitational force - with not a speck of dirt falling back to earth.

And to back-up this train of thought, strange luminous objects - UFOs - were frequently reported hovering and manouvering over the areas where the holes were found. And to add to the mystery, a cow was near one of the holes ... and it had been mutilated with some sort of lazer technology. There was no blood near the animal and veins which would normally collapse were found intact ... and strangely, the rectum was 'cored out'.

So Switzerland had holes not only in its cheese. The holes in the earth have produced a mystery that no one as yet has explained fully. And, until they do ... the alien UFO must remain the answer for many people.

And it is true to say that governments know much more then they are prepared to say ... about space aliens and UFOs.

SEX

So let us end Ghost Stations V on a lighter note and, what better than Sex. My old and, dear friend in Canada, Herb Currotte wrote to say he was sorry he, could not help out with any strange happenings. But, he could help out with advice for my Labrador dog that I am about to purchase at the time of writing.

It is such good advice that I must pass on his advice, on what not to name your dog. This is what he had to say:

Sergeant Currotte, Royal Canadian Air Force, seen here at Castletown in Scotland in December 1940. He poses near a Hurricane of No 1 Fighter Squadron.

‘Everybody who has a dog calls him ‘Rover.’ I call mine ‘Sex.’ He’s a great pal but he has caused me a great deal of embarrassment. When I went to city hall to renew his dog licence, I told the clerk I would like a licence for Sex.

‘I’d like one, too’, he said.

‘But this is a dog,’

He said he didn’t care what she looked like.

‘You don’t understand. I’ve had Sex since I was nine year old.’

He winked and said, ‘You must have been quite a lad.’

When I got married and went on my honeymoon, I took the dog with me. I told the motel clerk that I wanted a room for my wife and me and, a special room for Sex.

‘You don’t need a special room’, he said ‘As long as you pay your bill we don’t care what you do.’

‘Look, you don’t seem to understand, Sex keeps me awake at night.’

‘Funny - I have the same problem,’ replied the clerk.

One day I entered Sex in a contest but, before the competition began, the dog ran away. Another contestant asked me why I was just standing there, looking disappointed. I told him I had planned to have Sex in the Contest. He told me I should have sold my own tickets.

‘But you don’t understand,’ I said, ‘I had hoped to have Sex on T.V.’

‘Now that cable is all over the place it’s no big deal anymore,’ he replied with a shrug.

When my wife and I separated, we went to court to fight for custody of the dog, I said,

‘Your Honour, I had Sex before I was married,’ I blurted out.

‘The courtroom isn’t a confessional, stick to the case, please,’ snapped the Judge.

Then I told him that after I was married, Sex left me.

‘Me, too, he replied.

Last night Sex ran off again. I spent hours looking around town for him. A cop came over to me and asked: ‘What are you doing in this alley at four o'clock in the morning?'... I told him that I was looking for Sex. My case comes up Monday ... Your Canadian friend - Herb Currotte.

Fifty years on ... 1990 ... former Flight Sergeant Herb Currotte - far left as looking at picture - still wearing a forage-cap, takes part in a television show commemorating the Battle of Britain. And, with a dog named Sex, you would expect Herb to be sitting next to a female beauty. 'Feminine pulchritude,' he said 'that is beauty in ordinary English ... at their request, of course.' And he added with a cheeky grin, 'Sex, Sex, Sex.'

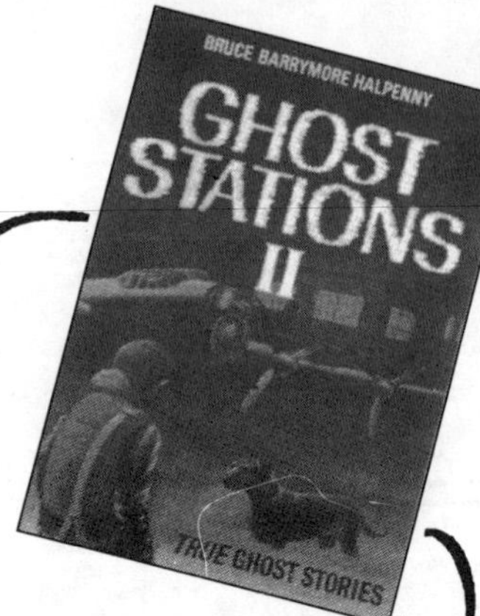

Other books.....

.....from the Master Pen

of

Bruce Barrymore - Halpenny

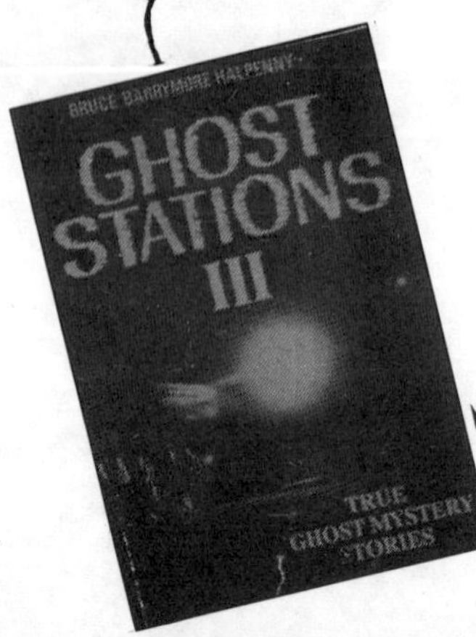

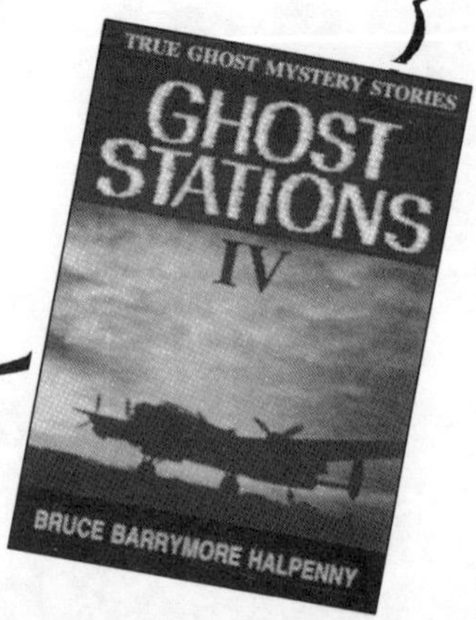